Who's Got Your Back?

Who's Got Your Back?

MAKING AND KEEPING GREAT
FRIENDSHIPS AMONG MEN

David W. Smith

CrossLink Publishing

CrossLink Publishing
1601 Mt. Rushmore Rd, STE 3288
Rapid City, SD 57702

Ordering Information:
Quantity sales. Special discounts are available on quantity purchases by corporations, associations, and others. For details, contact the "Special Sales Department" at the address above.

Who's Got Your Back?/Smith —1st ed.

ISBN 978-1-63357-173-0

Library of Congress Control Number: 2019936880

First edition: 10 9 8 7 6 5 4 3 2 1

What Others Have to Say about Who's Got Your Back?

David Smith's book, *Who's Got Your Back?*, reminds me of the writings of a seasoned craftsman who over the years has amassed a virtual tool chest of wisdom in regard to making and maintaining great relationships. This book is rich in understanding and insights, not only from Smith's own experience and research, but also from the lives of numerous other authors, not to mention his countless references from the ultimate book on relationships, the Bible itself. I highly recommend that you take the time to read, ponder, and most importantly, apply these principles to your own circle of friends as well as those whom you may add to your list by becoming their friend.

—David Ravenhill, author of Welcome Home: Receiving the Father's Forgiveness and Acceptance, pastor and itinerant Bible teacher

This good book will bring into sharp focus a genuine and functional and real-life definition of manliness. Dr. David Smith has skillfully woven stories with practical application strategies into a narrative that promotes clarity as to how we ought to live our lives. Streamed throughout the book are the desired character traits and values that we feel are a necessity to build and support trusting relationships. Consider this as a blueprint for not only building friendships with others but a way to bring happiness and success to our personal and professional lives.

—Gary Smit, Ed.D., dean of faculty, Josephson Institute of Ethics

David Smith is a humble practitioner of friendships, and for five decades I have been blessed to experience the integrity and joyful generosity of his life! We first met when I was a student in his classroom. He and his wife have pursued intentional connection with me ever since, and their thoughtful and caring ways continue to enrich me and my family. This work captures the depth of David's research as a historian and sociologist, and as a theologian who studies the Scriptures and lives them. The stories he shares from his own life and those he's gathered from others empower us all with the possibilities of life-giving friendships.
—**Margo Balsis, senior staff member for The Navigators at Purdue University**

David Smith has been a gracious friend and encourager for over twenty years. I appreciate his consistent servant-leadership in the public sector including his service as an effective superintendent of our public high school system. His new book, *Who's Got Your Back?*, articulates the clarion call that men today be the kind of men that Jesus modeled for us. David shows us how we can be strong, task-oriented, and achieving but also warm-hearted and unmistakably relationship-driven. David understands the rough and tumble of everyday life that most of us experience and provides us with an abundance of practical ways to sidestep negative societal norms while equipping us to establish mutually satisfying friendships.
—**David Riemenschneider, Th.D., founder and lead pastor, Bloomingdale Church, Bloomingdale, Illinois**

What made David Smith's *Who's Got Your Back?* special for me is that it builds bridges between biblical truth and modern behavioral science. The author combines a lifetime of personal experience, the research skills of a sociologist, and his Christian faith to create a wonderful men's guidebook for building better human relationships. This is a "must read" for any man who feels isolated from those around him who should be an important part of his life. While the book focuses primarily on creating healthy relationships between men, it offers many helpful anecdotes on marriage and parenting, as well.

—Charles Dunn, Ph.D., history professor, teacher, author of *The Nurse and the Navigator: A Son's Memoir of His Parents' Battlefield Romance*

Men need to be in meaningful relationships with other men. Strength, vision, character, and priorities become clear when you're doing life with other guys. When you're flying solo, you make mistakes and no one is there to hold you accountable. David Smith's new book shows in realistic ways how men should and can form great friendships. Women, buy it for your man and he will make his relationship with you a higher priority!

—Jay Payleitner, national speaker and best-selling author of *52 Things Wives Need from Their Husbands* and *What If God Wrote Your Bucket List?*

Who's Got Your Back? has a finger on the pulse of modernity. Real friendships can be the antidote to alienation in our fast-paced world. Dr. David Smith offers his timeless guide with vital meaningful principles, based on his own experience, research, and faith for the blessings and enrichment that true friends bring mankind.

—Ilona Garrett, author, teacher, member, and presenter, International Press Club of Chicago

David Smith has written a very enjoyable and practical book, Who's Got your Back? that is full of memorable stories about what it is like in this day and age to have someone special in your life. Every person needs others in their life. David describes the important "how-tos" when analyzing why and who should be on our team. These genuine friendships within our inner circle

complete us in our quest for the purpose that God has created us to become.
—**Darrel Billups, Th.D., emeritus executive director,** *National Coalition Ministries to Men* **(NCMM)**

It is an informative experience to read the intimate stories and practical and engaging insights that David Smith shares throughout *Who's Got Your Back?* Reading this book will enhance and make more enjoyable our personal relationships. His new book helps us to appreciate better how we can improve our communication and relationship skills. David unravels the mystery behind the reason communication often breaks down. He gives us the tools needed to make and keep great friendships as we relate more effectively with other people. This is a good book for all of us, not just for men.
—**Glady Sander, RN, camp nurse at Phantom Ranch Bible Camp, and counselor at Willow Pioneer Ministry for special needs adults**

This book is dedicated to my son, Cameron,
and to my daughter, Julie.

Contents

Preface

After several years of living on the north side of Chicago, my family and I prepared for a career move to suburban Indianapolis. I was surprised that my "good-byes" to my friends and neighbors were casual, even perfunctory, and lacking in any feeling, while my wife, Sue Ann's "good-byes" to her friends were heartfelt and meaningful and included hugs and tears and genuine commitments to stay close. I wondered if this was just about me or whether most men had similar superficial relationship experiences. I decided this was an important question for me, but not just for me—and so began a journey of discovery about why men have few if any close friends and what can we do to change that and begin to make great friendships that can last a lifetime.

Through the years, I have shared as a conference speaker and writer in books and articles my concern about the largely friendless condition of most men. Since those earlier days, the problem of men living lonely, emotionally barren lives seems to have only gotten worse. I encourage men to do genuine day-by-day relationship-building that candidly deals with the important theme of *Who's Got Your Back?* The title might not be as grammatically proper, but I thought it was a bit catchier than asking *Who Has Your Back?*

Acknowledgments

I'm grateful for those who have shared with me their thoughts about forming meaningful and satisfying connections with other people. I appreciate their openness and candor. I want to express my appreciation to the strangers who took the time to talk with me and to complete a questionnaire. There was much to learn from these individuals and from their straightforward, candid comments. It was fun and informative to talk with friends and strangers alike. Thank you, too, for the generous comments about this book that those who know me well have freely volunteered. I appreciate and have benefited from many practical proposal and outline suggestions I received from my literary agent, Gary Foster. And I certainly acknowledge my indebtedness to my dear wife and closest of friends, Sue Ann Smith. Without her support and patience, this book would not have reached what hopefully is a successful conclusion. I'm grateful for her willingness to listen, discuss, and comment on an endless list of topics.

Introduction

One of the greatest indicators of our emotional and spiritual health is how well we're connected with others. Who has your back? Who can count on you? We fall short, rarely because of a lack of some knowledge or ability. We often fail in our personal and work experiences because of our inability to connect well with others. No one plans to lead a mediocre life; it just happens. We're more likely to form alliances than we are friendships. We don't seem to mean much to each other anymore. It doesn't have to be that way.

This book is about a real-life positive and practical journey to form enjoyable and genuine and spiritual relationships in every area of life. It's no surprise that those who have your back will usually be the same individuals who know they can count on you in the good times and in times of trouble. It may seem counterintuitive, but giving to others is often more satisfying than receiving from others.

It's the individuals we're close to who make life worth living.

I'm curious about and committed to learning more about friendships. I wonder about questions like these: What kind of friends do you have? Are they work friends, sports friends, or neighborhood friends? How about friendships at church? Recent Pew Research reveals that only about one in five men attends religious services weekly. Whom would you turn to if your whole world caved in? Whom would you trust enough to share your intimate thoughts, fears, and frustrations? Who in your life would drop everything to help you during a difficult time?

How many friends do people have? What's your definition of friendship? Does the Bible offer practical advice for creating friendships? How do friends think and behave? Why do women typically have more friends than men? Why are friendships with the opposite sex so rare? How does age and marital status affect friendships? Why do some friendships fall apart? What's involved in making and keeping satisfying and worthwhile relationships?

To learn more about close friendships, I read as many of the secular and faith-based publications I could find. This was useful, but what was also very helpful for real life was when I conducted my own interviews, usually with strangers. While I interviewed friends and neighbors and guys at work, most of the slightly more than four hundred conversations I had were with strangers who were willing to talk with me in a neutral setting, often at a shopping center. Strangers were usually very honest, I found. They had no image or reputation to protect since they'd likely never see me again. What they told me was often surprising and I believe important. I continue to ask the opinions of others at conferences and retreats when I'm invited to give presentations. I've shared much in the following chapters from what I learned from many candid conversations and from my own life experiences. I'm therefore less formal; I've decided to make this book more like a conversation with less attention devoted to a formal bibliography and cited notes.

CHAPTER 1

Who Needs Friends?

Two are better than one....
—Ecclesiastes 4:9

*A friend is one of the nicest things you can have
and one of the best things you can be.*
—Douglas Pagels

Chuck was one of the hardest-working marketing representatives in his software company's history. He was married and had two children, both of whom had done well in school. Chuck spent so much time working and winning in the marketplace that he had little time and energy to spend developing friendships or networking with others. Certainly, he knew many people at work, and he came in contact daily with clients who relied on him and his expertise. But no one really knew Chuck. He was so busy achieving, it appeared that what he did for a living was his total identity. If he wasn't working with a client, he was developing sales pitches and problem-solving ideas that would attract future clients. Nothing else seemed to matter.

He finally walked out of the office after receiving a grand sendoff retirement party. He had worked hard in a rapidly changing industry for over thirty years. Now he looked forward to enjoying the wealth and prestige he had acquired over the years. But he ended up enjoying it largely alone. Frustrated and disappointed from years of neglect, his wife had little interest in trying to build a new life together in retirement. And his children, who had since become adults and left home to begin their own lives, rarely connected with him in any meaningful way.

Chuck tried to keep up a few relationships he had previously with some of his former coworkers. A few former colleagues he knew would get together with him to talk shop, but after a while they had less time for him since he soon was out of touch with technological, social media, and market changes and the rapidly changing base of clients. Within a short year after his retirement, Chuck became a stranger at the company where he had spent so many years diligently working. Feeling unwanted and unneeded, he stopped reaching out. Calls and emails and texts from his kids also became less frequent. Chuck was largely alone and unhappy.

* * *

Jerry hunted, fished, and did all of the maintenance and most of the repair work on his truck. He helped out at his church sometimes, doing repairs on donated cars that were fixed up and given to those in need, often to single mothers. On his construction job he was reliable and got along all right with the other workers. He dated once in a while, and a couple of nights a week went out with some of his work buddies to a nearby sports bar.

Jerry was easy to talk to, but his conversations were limited to safe topics such as work, cars, and sports. When Jerry was diagnosed with lung cancer, most of those who heard about it didn't know what to say. And when he had difficult monthly chemotherapy treatments, except for occasional and brief visits from his pastor, no one came to see him or offered to drive him to and from the hospital. Eighteen months later, when Jerry died, a few guys he knew carried his casket. A former girlfriend came to the funeral, and his pastor delivered a short eulogy. His funeral was brief, and the tears shed were few. Jerry died pretty much alone.

* * *

When someone had a problem, they felt they could call Frank. Sick and in the hospital? Frank would be the one who would make a visit. Marital problems? Frank was good with helpful advice. Frank was "Mr. Fix-it." But whom could Frank really talk to? As the church's pastor, Frank knew that everyone needed friends, and he had tried to become friends with a few men he knew. Some of the men on his own small church elder board were not comfortable with his attempts to build friendships with them. Several felt uncomfortable being open and candid about their own life struggles. Frank seemed somehow all together and might think less of them if he actually knew more about their real lives.

Frank gave up trying to develop close contact with others. He tried to pour out his needs and concerns to God in prayer, but his need for companionship, his need for friendships, went largely unmet.

Chuck, Jerry, and Frank were all successful in many ways, and they knew many people, at least superficially, but they didn't have anyone they could really connect with, be open with, or count on in a time of need. There wasn't much joy and genuine connection with others. Many of us can identify with the circumstances of these three guys. Most of the time we don't think much about the quality of our relationships. Loneliness is widespread and getting worse and is possibly as dangerous a health risk as are smoking and obesity.

This book is for men, and also for the women who know men who are lacking quality personal relationships. I want to encourage men to see their need for friends and to show how they can enrich their lives and the lives of others by making and maintaining quality friendships. Most women actively seek friendships, nurture them, and benefit from and enjoy them. Men, on the other hand, usually don't make friends very well and don't know how to manage a friendship if they do make a friend. The relationships most men have with other men are limited generally to a coworker or buddy relationship, rather than an actual friendship.

What Is Friendship?˙

American author Ralph Waldo Emerson once said, "A friend is a person with whom one can be sincere." Maybe that means having someone you can share with and really discuss things that are important to you. The individuals who come to mind when you consider the question "who's got your back?" may well be your friends. I asked my wife, Sue Ann, for her definition of friendship. She thought for a moment and then smiled and simply responded, "Lois." Friendship to Sue Ann is a personal experience that exemplifies far more than a one-sentence or one-paragraph definition.

One example of male friendship is found in the historical biblical record of 1 Samuel 18:1–3; 19:1–7; and 23:15–18. We learn about a relationship that ran deep between Jonathan, the king's son, and David, a shepherd boy who later would surprisingly become the king of Israel. Their friendship was strong, built solidly on an inward attachment and personal commitment, rather than on any outward social status. The King James translation of the Bible records that "...the soul of Jonathan was knit with the soul of David..." (1 Samuel 18:1, KJV). These two men demonstrated a mutual acceptance of and concern for each other despite their very different social backgrounds. Their mutual promise to "watch each other's back" was born of an unconditional concern for each other (1 Samuel 18:3) during a very dangerous situation concerning Jonathan's father, King Saul. David and Jonathan were dependent upon each other (1 Samuel 23:15–16). Mutuality and respect, not individualism or competition, marked their friendship. Other positive friendships found in the Bible include Moses and Aaron; Elijah and Elisha; and the women Naomi and Ruth. We'll look in every chapter ahead at how friendship traits found in the Bible are best identified and lived out in our modern-day, hectic lives.

Friendship involves a concern for and involvement with the well-being of another. Friendship so defined seems to be hard to find. According to our cultural values, real men are encouraged to be competitive, non-emotional, strong with few insecurities, and able to deal largely alone with problems that come their way. You shouldn't "need" a friend, some might say. To need a friend, actor and former California governor Arnold Schwarzenegger believes, makes one a so-called girly man. But in spite of this cultural, go-it-alone bravado, it's nevertheless true that a joyful life and quality friendships are highly correlated. Depressive symptoms, including a reduced enjoyment with normal daily activities, are also correlated with friendlessness. So how did we get into this sorry situation of friendlessness, and what can we now do about it?

Friendship Made Personal

Do you have friends who have your back? Can others count on you in time of need? How we answer questions and deal with the issues associated with friendships can be life-changing. Phil McGraw, in his book *Life Code*, says it's essential to create a passionate nucleus of supporters. We need to find and bond with a core group of lifelong friends and supporters. Dr. Phil acknowledges that while difficult to accomplish, "we all need people we can truly trust and rely on, who cheer us on and truly want us to succeed. If you want a good friend, be a good friend."1

There is a sense of belonging and joy and positive change that can result because of our looking together at friendship. This should be fun. This review about friendship together is surely not about rules and regulations and a bunch of do's and don'ts. I hope you'll find within the following pages an enjoyable journey, and I'd welcome hearing from you and learning your thoughts and reactions after you've finished reading. My contact information is listed at the end of the book.

Focusing on Friendship Principles

I believe there are seven essential principles concerning friendship. These principles will form a major focus of our discussion throughout the book. These fundamental ideas are summarized as follows:

1. Friendships in which we both give and receive are essential to our spiritual and emotional well-being.
2. Most men lack friends of the heart and soul but can learn to improve the quality of their interpersonal relationships.
3. Most men lead lives that conform largely to our macho-dominated, twenty-first-century culture rather than to the masculine standards found in Scripture.
4. Women tend to experience more fulfilling friendships than men, and the reasons for this difference are not just biological.
5. Biblical principles of friendship can be identified and, when implemented, can change lives in a positive way.
6. Those who have close, nurturing friendships usually have many personality traits in common.
7. With the decline in the social stability of the extended family and even the nuclear family, friendships are becoming more important than ever before for the maintenance of emotional and spiritual health.

We will look at the validity of these seven principles to see how they apply to men in general and each of us individually. How do friendships develop? What are the basic personality traits of a good friend? What principles of friendship are offered in the Bible? How do age, marital status, and religion affect friendships? What can women do to help men form and maintain satisfying friendships? What can men do to help themselves in this important area of their lives?

Writers have made available abundant information dealing with marriage, family, sexuality, in-laws, work, and countless other topics. And yet little knowledge and few publications exist that provide us with an understanding of the dynamics of friendships. Most everyone has opinions about friendships, but few people have conducted actual research or candid interviews, or looked closely at the principles found in the Bible.

I mentioned earlier that in preparing to write this book, I assembled my own ideas and life experiences about men and friendship and read what others have written. I also spoke with dozens of my friends and acquaintances and also total strangers about this neglected topic.

I enjoyed talking with these people. And I think they enjoyed talking with me about the important subject of relationships. I talked with both men and women, young and old, rich and poor, married and not yet married, single and divorced, well-educated and not so well-educated, religious and not so religious. I asked strangers if they would mind taking a brief few minutes to give their answers on a questionnaire dealing with friendship. The survey I put together to share with them is shown below.

Friendship Research Survey

I am conducting research dealing with the topic of friendship. I welcome your comments. Thank you for taking time to express your opinions about the issues listed below.
David W. Smith

Questions for Men and Women

1. Please define the term **close friend.**

2. How many close friends do you have who fit the definition of a close friend you listed above?

_____Same sex

_____Opposite sex

3. Are you satisfied with the quality and quantity of your friendships? Please explain.

4. What can you do to begin and improve friendships and relationships with others?

5. Do you and your close friends share similar beliefs and interests (for example, in religion, politics, values, or hobbies)?

6. What are your personal obligations or responsibilities in a friendship?

I would welcome any other general comments you would like to share, and again, thank you for your involvement with this research. Here's my email contact: SDS894@yahoo.com

* * *

Much of what I learned from the personal responses collected from this survey is reported here in the book. I don't claim that my efforts at data collection and interpretation were particularly scientific, but I enjoyed the process and found the results quite interesting. I look forward to sharing with you simply in the on-going narrative what I discovered from the good people I had the chance to meet and talk with about friendships. I also asked respondents for their personal background information, which included their sex, age, marital status, income, occupation, education level, and religion. I thought you'd find this information interesting, so I've listed it next in percentages.

Survey Results of Personal Background

Gender		Age		Marital Status	
Male	47%	8-25	15%	Married	38%
Female	53%	26-35	18%	Single	23%
		36-45	24%	Divorced	22%
		46-55	19%	Remarried	9%
		56-65	12%	Widowed	8%
		66+	12%		

Income		Education	
Under $25,000	16%	High school or less	27%
$25,000-$45,000	37%	Some College	27%
$45,000-$65,000	31%	College Graduate	33%
$65,000+	17%	Graduate School	13%

Religion		Occupation	
Protestant	49%	Professional	13%
Catholic	29%	White Collar	18%
Jewish	6%	Blue Collar	40%
Other	9%	Other	29%
None	7%		

A Personal Note

I've written this book not so much as a dispassionate observer but more as one who has experienced the frustrations of unrealized, unfulfilled, and broken relationships. I have also known the joy, satisfaction, and responsibility that comes with a close friendship. More of what and who I am is revealed in these pages than I had originally intended. Like most men, I am somewhat reticent about revealing much of my true self, but writing a book about male friendship required, it seemed to me, that I be as honest and as open as possible.

I want to share with you from my experiences and the experiences of others. I have tried to avoid offering a simple, hackneyed, or dogmatic formula for improving relationships. This book represents a part of my own search for better relationships. Much of who I am still gets in the way of my giving to and receiving from friendships. What I am is simply a fellow pilgrim searching for and trying to contribute to relationships that become rewarding and satisfying.

I believe we are capable of relationships that bring joy and pleasure. Physical, emotional, and spiritual health is related to how well we are connected to others. We don't have to be lonely or go through life with a John Wayne, James Bond, Clint Eastwood, or some other tough guy mentality of macho solo independence. So I hope you'll read further to explore the real world of the close, satisfying relationships we are meant to enjoy.

Discussion Questions

1. What are your thoughts about the seven principles of friendship listed in this chapter?

2. Are there any of the statements listed within the seven principles you might disagree with or are not sure should be considered as part of a basic principle?

Why Are We Lacking in Close Friendships?

We take care of our health, we lay up money, to make our roof tight, and our clothing sufficient, but who provides wisely that he shall not be wanting in the best property of all—friends?
—Ralph Waldo Emerson

As iron sharpens iron, so one person sharpens another.
—Proverbs 27:17

Men are different from women, for which we all give thanks. Unfortunately, however, some of the differences between the sexes are not so positive. One difference is the way in which we perceive relationships. Our thinking about friends is often unlike that of our female counterparts. Researchers, including Herb Goldberg and Lisa Wade1 at Salon.com, asked adult men if they had any close friends and found that many seemed surprised by the question. "No. Why? Should I?" was a common response. I found the same results from the interviews and conversations I conducted. Perhaps men perceive their isolation, their lack of genuine relationships, as normal.

What's going on? Why don't men make, keep, and nurture relationships very well? Some distinctly male characteristics are, of course, natural and good, while others tend to be harmful (see

Chapter 5). These first few chapters explore why many men live in a way that hinders the making and keeping of close and enjoyable friendships. I've thought about some of the barriers to true friendship among men I'd like to share with you.

The Male Aversion to Showing Emotions

Early in life, boys receive cultural messages that they are not supposed to show emotions. Expressing feelings is generally taboo for males. From an early age, even in our modern age, boys still hear the words "Don't be a sissy"; "Big boys don't cry"; "Aren't you a little too old to be sitting on your mother's lap?" The message comes through loud and clear—boys must learn to be men, and real men should conceal many of their affections and emotions. Some millennials and Generation Z men feel they are better at expressing emotions than their fathers. We'll have to wait and see.

Years ago, Americans saw on network television the return of many war-ravaged prisoners from Vietnam. Some of these former POWs had not been seen by family or friends for several years. Many relatives had feared the worst—that the one they loved and missed so much might have been killed. Therefore, the long-hoped-for reunions were packed with emotion. Yet mothers often reacted differently from fathers as they saw their sons for the first time, perhaps in years. Mothers and wives were open with their expressions of emotion, but with just a few exceptions, fathers were more reserved. I watched one father simply extend his hand to the son he had not seen in years.

One of my friends from high school, Mark, fought in Vietnam and was seriously injured and nearly died. And now, all these years later, he will say it remains difficult to trust anyone and to become close to someone. Today many men and women defending our nation's interests in the Middle East and in many other places around the world return home often with physical and post-traumatic stress problems like those who fought in Vietnam and other wars. The adjustments of returning to civilian life can and often are overwhelming for our returning military personnel. I always look for opportunities to express gratitude to any veteran I have the privilege of meeting in daily life. A simple "Thank you for your service," can mean a lot.

Except for committing acts of violence or participating in contact sports, such as football and hockey, men do little touching of one another. Touching might imply sexual interest. The thought of hugging someone as a simple expression of affection or friendship without sexual overtones is, for many, somewhat complicated. Some men are embarrassed if they are hugged by a friend.

Perhaps some men shun physical expressions of emotional feelings by other men because of an unconscious fear of latent gay tendencies. This may be true even in our modern time when gay identification and marriage have become more mainstream, including in decisions by the U.S. Supreme Court. Nevertheless, boys generally learn that males don't affectionately touch and hug each other, and fathers tend to hug and express closeness more with their daughters than sons.

Inability to Fellowship

The simple request, "Let's have lunch together," may be followed with the response, "Sure, what's up?" This exchange seems to make it clear that an independent man doesn't really need the company of another man. We may manufacture non-emotional reasons for being together. A business deal must be discussed, or a game must be played or watched. Men may use drinking or sports or work as an excuse to gather together. Rarely do men plan a meeting together solely because they have a desire to simply share each other's company.

Even when the same men are frequently together socially, their interactions may remain at a superficial level. Just how long can conversations mainly limited to politics and sports be nourishing to the human spirit? And talking with someone today about political issues can become something like a contact sport. The same male employees can have lunch together for years and still limit their conversation to sports, politics, cars, and attempts at humor.

Inadequate Role Models

Two decades into the twenty-first century, and we are still beset with Rambo-style models for manhood. Our television and movie heroes help to perpetuate the male problem of aloneness. Heroes tend to be self-sufficient, strong, and impersonal. They usually avoid long-range emotional entanglements. Through the years, characters such as those portrayed by James Cagney, John Wayne, Clint Eastwood, Sean Connery, Sylvester Stallone, Tom Selleck, Arnold Schwarzenegger, Al Pacino, Denzel Washington, Brad Pitt, Leonardo DiCaprio, Hugh Jackson, Mark Sinclair, Tom Cruise, George Clooney, and Johnny Depp are examples of hard, independent men who use and sometimes abuse rather than love both women and men. And perceived "real men" tend to neglect or ignore children. Even in the twenty-first century, men who spend too much time with kids are believed to be somehow less manly. Our elementary public and private schools still have difficulty finding qualified male teachers for the younger primary grades.

Our masculine role models are usually independent and strong and can stand alone when there are problems. In the classic western film *High Noon*, actor Gary Cooper epitomized American masculinity in a supreme display of bravery. When he was challenged, the woman he loved implored him to avoid the fight and leave town, but he felt he had no choice. While all others turned away in cowardice, Cooper's character, a frontier marshal, stood alone to defend the small town against a gang of thugs. This image of manliness, of going it alone, is quite rigid and difficult to live up to in real life.

Our media heroes are often violent and seem to be always interested in sex. Many television programmers have added displays of gratuitous sex to attract viewers. The low-cost production of the TV shows *The Bachelor* and *The Young and the Restless* are shameful examples. Commercial television continues to develop so-called action shows that often display disdain for marriage and committed love and instead show a continual interest in casual sex and violence. Such programming both leads and reflects public opinion.

Commercial network shows like *Revenge, How to Get Away with Murder, Hawaii Five-O, Killer Women, Scandal,* and *Blacklist* are examples of the public's tolerance for and even fascination with violence and casual sex. Much cable programming is as bad and often worse than the commercial offerings including shows like *Wife Swap, Paradise Hotel, Temptation Island* and *Lindsay Lohan's Beach Club.* Much of the graphic video game products are saturated with sexual violence. How does the hero solve problems? He gets angry and becomes violent. One learns that problems can be solved quickly by physical action. The average television show is sixty or ninety minutes in length. Patience, compromise, and long-suffering are seldom traits of the celebrated masculine characters in these programs.

These models of toughness have led many men to respond to real or imagined challenges to their manliness in ways that may be harmful. They are quick to respond to a dare, or what seems to be an insult to their pride. Who participates in barroom brawls? Who engages in road rage and tries to cut off another motorist on the road? Who commits drive-by and school shootings? Who commits domestic violence? Who engages in shouting matches or trades insults? Is it any wonder that men have a life expectancy that is several years less than women? Of course, women are capable of physical violence as well, but usually men are the ones who may more quickly get angry and even turn to violence to settle a perceived slight or a dispute.

Sadly, this mask of aggressiveness and strength tends to keep us men from knowing ourselves or each other. Fears, joys, loves, hopes, and concerns are largely kept concealed within, hindering us from forming close friendships.

Inordinately Competitive

Men feel they have to excel at what they do. If a man plays a game, he feels he must win. When Jimmy Carter was the president of the United States, he played baseball with the press corps. The competition was intense. President Carter really wanted his team to win. Carter also concerned himself daily with White House tennis court action. He wanted to know who had played whom and the outcome of each match. Winning was very important to him.

Former President Obama enjoys playing basketball and golf. When he gets to play, he is very competitive and wants to win. John Kennedy's sister, Eunice Shriver, described how her brother hated to lose at anything. In fact, "The only thing Jack ever got emotional about was losing."

Winning is very important to men. My former neighbor Alan and I were good tennis players, but Alan was just a little better than I and always made a point of giving me his best game. One summer we played once or twice a week. I never won a single set. I always lost. It was important for Alan to win. I tried to rationalize the situation by saying the exercise was good for me, but deep down I resented losing each and every set on each and every outing.

Parents often compare the personal achievements of their sons with the accomplishments of other boys. A boy learns that other boys are his competitors and, therefore, potential adversaries. This kind of thinking works to undermine the development of close relationships among men and boys.

Competition is very highly respected between men. Vince Lombardi, the great Green Bay Packers football coach, used to say, "Winning isn't everything; it's the only thing." Many coaches as well as corporate executives have held to the belief that nice guys finish last. Bobby Knight, the former basketball coach at Indiana University and Texas Tech, has been criticized for motivating his teams with fear, swearing, yelling, and other forms of inappropriate and undisciplined behavior. Many come to his defense with the simple statement, "But he wins and that's what is important." In other words, the end justifies the means. If you can win, all else is acceptable. For the record, a coach can win without the display of poor behavior. A favorite example of winning while demonstrating honorable behavior is John Wooden, who for years coached men's basketball at UCLA.

Men generally find it difficult simply to have fun. It's hard for us to set aside the burden of needing to win. I find it difficult to fully enjoy a game of tennis unless I win. I think I'm a good player. Of course, there's nothing wrong with friendly competition, but men may become so uptight about beating the competition that they often miss out on the joy of participation and the simple fun of being with friends. If men are not good at a sport or an activity, they'll likely avoid it entirely. Why do we have to win at what we do? What if we are not the greatest athlete, singer, trombone player, or whatever? Let's just do some activities to have fun and fellowship.

This notion about the priority of winning extends to mental areas as well as physical. Most men are reluctant to admit to ignorance about a topic. To do so might leave the impression that they cannot compete or are less than all-knowing. During my first year as a public high school teacher, I labored under the false belief that, as a teacher and as a man, I should have most of the answers to students' questions. Luckily for me, and my students, I soon realized there was nothing wrong with saying, "I don't know." This freed me from the burden of trying to be a walking encyclopedia. The students and I could learn some things together. And now, of course, if we don't know some fact, we can "Google" the question and usually get an answer quickly.

Students won't let you play the all-knowing game anyway. They'll press you for more answers and think or even say, "Who are you kidding?" The know-it-all approach keeps others at arm's length.

When my family was living in a northern suburb of Chicago, we had a neighbor who tried to convey the impression that he was intelligent and knew virtually everything, regardless of the topic. He became especially forceful in expounding his religious and political opinions at neighborhood block parties, which were conducted on many summer weekends on our dead-end street. If we disagreed with his chauvinistic ideas, he could become upset.

Most men, to some extent, want to be in command of whatever they are doing, be it with sports or in a conversation. A family relative of Theodore Roosevelt, speaking of the former president, said, "He wants to be the bride at every wedding and the corpse at every funeral." Most of us want to be in control to the extent that our behavior might present a barrier to positive relationships.

Unwillingness to Ask for Help

We seem to be reluctant to seek help for anything from an ailing marriage to an ailing physical body. Men are reluctant to share problems not only with counselors and physicians and other professionals, but even with their own wives and families. If asked why he refuses to share a concern, a man usually responds that he doesn't have a problem or that he doesn't want to burden the family or friend with his problems. I know I don't want to bother anyone with whatever I'm dealing with.

This resistance to admitting dependency on others is not limited to the major emotional areas of our lives. A cousin of mine attempted to give road directions to her brother-in-law during a trip to a family reunion. This was before everyone had GPS for navigation. The brother-in-law refused to listen and proceeded to drive on in the wrong direction for at least ten minutes. The sister-in-law was furious. "If you don't want to listen to me," she said, "at least stop at a gas station and ask a stranger for directions." Finally, he did just that, but by stopping at a filling station, this man was admitting that he needed help. The family members in the car expected to hear him say, "I'm sorry, I made a mistake." However, that was too much for this guy to say, so the carload of relatives drove off, finally in the correct direction, toward their family reunion—in silence.

Boys learn early to stand on their own two feet. "Don't count on others" or "God helps those who help themselves" are comments of masculine advice. Boys who cling too much to parents are potential sources of embarrassment. When my father was five or six years old, his father took him to the end of a pier in Chicago, threw him into Lake Michigan, and said simply, "Swim." Later he added, "You must learn to take care of yourself." Sadly, what my father learned instead was not to trust his dad and perhaps not to really trust any man. We can have too much self-sufficiency, which may rob us of the fulfillment of our need for and enjoyment with the support, love, and concern of friends and loved ones.

Incorrect Priorities

Men often have a distorted order of priorities. Physical things are more important than relationships. Status is obtained by the acquisition of material wealth rather than, say, the number of close friends. I heard of a man who often demonstrated disrespect for his wife's comments and attitudes by responding, "That's immaterial," to something she might say. It seems so strange that love, concern, and relationships should take second place to the material emphasis of so many men.

This distortion of emphasis on the material is certainly not a recent development. The Old Testament prophet Haggai, in chapter 1:3–11 for example, warned that we are more concerned about living in paneled houses (material things) than we are about our relationship with God and our fellow man (immaterial things).

In the New Testament, we can find a similar lesson in the parable of the rich fool (Luke 12:15–20), which has several appropriate applications for us today. The man in the parable, for example, was a fool because of his inordinate emphasis on materialism at the expense of developing close relationships with others; his belief that his belongings were his own and were the measure of self-worth and importance; his preoccupation with storing instead of sharing; and his idea that he could feed his soul with bread. This lifestyle makes no sense to God. That's why Jesus called the man a fool.

The rich fool would likely feel at home within our Western-oriented society. Our culture usually rejects and even ridicules the criteria God has established for us men in our dealings with others. God's measure of a man is Christlike love (1 Corinthians 13:1–3), which produces a servant's heart and behavior (Matthew 20:25–27). If we would only discover that God wants us to be concerned less about ourselves and more about others, we would live our lives to the fullest by embracing a masculinity that is more like Jesus. Unfortunately, a man's success is still largely determined and measured by how much wealth and power and influence can be acquired, often at the expense of intimacy and fellowship with his family and friends and coworkers.

The problem of a lack of closeness and intimacy exists even in our churches. In church we sit together and sing together, and we greet one another pleasantly when we arrive or when we leave at the end of a service. We do all these things, sometimes for years, without forming any real personal connections or relationships. The church, therefore, becomes a place where Christians may reside together but feel emotionally alone.

I heard at church of a man dying of a rare disease. His name appears in the church bulletin under the heading "Remember in Prayer." The deaconesses sent him flowers, and periodically someone, usually the pastor, would offer a public prayer on his behalf. But to my knowledge, few if any men in the church had gone to spend quality time with him, to listen and to share, in short, to be his friend. The Bible teaches us that, as we have opportunity, we are to do good unto all men (Galatians 6:10). Instead we manage to insulate ourselves from the healthy and the sick alike.

I met a fellow public school superintendent, Dr. Donald Draayer from Minnesota, when we both worked as consultants for a national energy company. He once said that after he retired he joined a men's Bible study group and he went early and remained after his Rotary meetings and sometimes looked for local dinner outings with other men because he knew that good relationships were so important for good health. Don said that "relationships are a powerful component in all human affairs." When Morrie Schwartz was dying of Lou Gehrig's Disease, one of his students, Mitch Albom, visited with him weekly. Mitch appreciated greatly his teacher and the privilege to meet and learn from him during his final several months of life. Their conversations resulted in the bestselling book *Tuesdays with Morrie*. Mitch learned much from Morrie, including that while we need others to survive when we are very young, and usually when we are very old, the secret is the in-between years where we live most of our lives when we truly need others as well.

Patrick Morley, when a young businessman, made it a habit to always ask older men what their greatest regrets were, hoping he could learn some wise tips for his own life. Many would lament, "...my children are grown and gone and I never really got to know them. Now they are too busy for me." Patrick, who is the founder of the *Man in the Mirror* ministry, believes that no amount of success at work can compensate for failure at home. He concludes that, "Many men are succeeding in their work but failing in life. So many of us are hurting silently with our relationships with our wives, children, parents, business associates, and friends. We can wound those we love the most."2 The pursuit of the so-called good life often results in broken, superficial, and neglected relationships. We can be like Humpty Dumpty when our relationships fall apart, and we struggle with the difficulty to look for ways to put it all back together.

We may know in our hearts and in our minds that we truly need others. Nevertheless, we also fear getting involved with others beyond a superficial level. This lack of intimacy is foreign to the biblical injunction to "bear one another's burdens, and so fulfill the law of Christ" (Galatians 6:2). There is no way to do this while keeping others at arm's length. The Galatians' letter (3:27–29) reminds us that we are to enjoy fellowship together, a oneness as believers in Christ. Even though the barriers that separate men are emotionally and spiritually destructive, they do exist and may even be becoming more formidable. Men pay a heavy price for their unwillingness or inability to remove the barriers that separate them and prevent the formation of close relationships. Too many of us still tend to believe the creed of the so-called masculine man: He shall not cry; he shall not display weakness. He shall not need affection. He shall comfort but not need or want comforting. He shall be needed but not need. He shall touch but not be touched. He shall be strong and secure and often stand alone.

A masculinity that is detached, unemotional, and uninvolved, lacking commitment, is not masculinity at all. We who have consciously or unconsciously assimilated a false masculinity have had to pay a heavy price. The emotional and physical consequences we have experienced are considered in the next chapter.

Discussion Questions

1. What prevents men from reaching out to others in friendship and fellowship? Do any of these explanations apply to you personally?

2. How important is winning to you? Discuss the positive and negative characteristics of a lifestyle based largely on competition.

3. How do you measure self-worth or the worth of another? What role do wealth, social influence, and physical strength have in how you define the value of yourself and others?

4. From what source or from whom did you acquire your standard of masculinity? Why do you think it is a standard worth living by? What benefits has it brought to you? What have been the negatives?

CHAPTER 3

The High Cost of Going It Alone

We have met the enemy and he is us.
—Walt Kelly in Pogo

But pity anyone who falls and has no one to help them up.
—Ecclesiastes 4:10

Modern men are conditioned mentally like cavemen of old, meant to slug it out alone with a saber-toothed tiger, and at the same time they are often less prepared to meet the constraints of living in our contemporary twenty-first-century world. We learn early in life to be competitive and sometimes combative, and few of us learn to relate well with others. Few of us value close interpersonal relationships, and fewer still seem willing to invest the time and emotional energy necessary for the development of closeness with others.

The increasing fragmentation of our community life, corporate pressures, the breakdown of the extended and even the nuclear family, the drive for success, the busyness of daily life, and the high rate of mobility have all taken a significant toll on the intimate relationships we might otherwise acquire and sustain.

How has all of this affected our quantity of life? The average life expectancy for an American is about eighty years; for men the figure is seventy-seven and for women it is eighty-two. Women therefore are living an average of five years longer than their male counterparts. In 2019, the U.S. life expectancy was reduced slightly for the second straight year, largely because of soaring drug overdose opiate deaths.

Not only do men on average not live as long as women, but there is more bad news. The fortunate men who do remain alive into old age tend to have more physical problems than women. The onetime strong, independent, competitive man is often, in old age, cared for by his wife or other family member. A twice divorced friend of mine from high school lives alone. Following a recent and painful knee surgery, he told me, "I'm looking for a nurse with a purse." Maybe it's no wonder his first two marriages failed. Most caregivers, whether close relatives or hired employees, are women.

Stress: Positive or Negative?

During the 1930s, Dr. Hans Selye first discovered the negative impact that stress has upon the human body. His work with hormones and the endocrine glands revealed a strong correlation between the way the mind and body work together. In the last nearly ninety years, several studies have confirmed the results from this early research.

As dangerous as stress can be, we need not fear the frequent pressure-packed moments of everyday living that so often create stress. Stressful experiences are a normal part of a person's social and work life. It is not so much the amount of stress one experiences that affects mental and physical health, but rather the manner in which one handles the stress. If your boss is difficult to work for, this is sure to produce anxiety and stress, but it doesn't have to affect your physical health or your feelings of self-worth and well-being.

One important key to harmlessly venting daily stress is a strong network of friends and family. Breaking close ties, such as in divorce for example, or never establishing intimate relationships in the first place, appears to increase a whole litany of health dangers, including heart disease, strokes, hypertension, migraine and tension headaches, rashes, ulcers, and even infectious diseases such as tuberculosis. If we are to avoid a potentially ruinous impact of these afflictions to our health, we need to share the frustration, stresses, loneliness, and anxieties of everyday life with individuals we love and who love us in return.

Cardiologists Meyer Friedman and Ray H. Rosenman in the 1950s were the first to identify and develop a list related to *Type A Behavior and Your Heart*, which includes numerous behavioral characteristics that appear in high-risk heart patients. They include a sense of time urgency, a persistent desire for recognition and advancement, a strong competitive drive, an emphasis on work at the expense of social and family relationships, and a tendency to take on excessive responsibilities because of the feeling that "only I can do it."

These damaging traits are usually associated with men rather than women. These are almost synonymous with what we have learned to believe is normal male behavior. Of course, women experience stress too, often in larger doses than men. Many women must juggle work and home responsibilities, yet they seem to adapt to stress and daily predicaments better than most men. It's about how we respond to stress rather than the stress itself that gives us our problems.

A study conducted by the University of California at Berkeley has shown that American men are among those who have the highest heart disease rates in the entire world. Japanese men, for example, have a much lower rate of coronary disease. Such variables as diet, smoking, and drinking were not as important as close emotional connections with others. Japan is a highly industrialized society, with a dense population living within a relatively small archipelago. There are approximately 127 million Japanese living in an area the size of California. Tension and stress from high expectations are present, but emphasis is placed on the importance of family and friends. Because of their priorities, the Japanese are able to defuse some of the stresses inherent in many industrialized jobs and societies.

In the past few years, the Japanese have become more like Americans and other countries from the West. One wonders how Japan will develop in the years ahead. In 2018, the babies were not coming in large numbers, and the Japanese government projects a population decline for years to come.

I have visited Japan several times, most recently in 2017 at a time when nearby North Korea was launching missiles into the Sea of Japan. This was, of course, very concerning to the Japanese, the United States and much of the world. I worked in Japan on U.S. Air Force bases, helping to evaluate U.S.-dependent schools. It has also been my privilege to host several Japanese educators when they were visiting the United States. I was impressed with their focused attention toward family and friends.

We in the United States tend to think in an "I" or "me" context, while the Japanese seem to support more of a "we" mindset. The Japanese seem more likely to view themselves as part of a group than as autonomous individuals. They are responsible to others and want to be in harmony with them. In the longevity game, it is the men with balanced lives who are more likely to live better and longer lives. They mix work with fun and connections to other people. Individuals who live long, happy lives are not one-dimensional. Retired University of Wisconsin expert on aging Dr. Roger J. Stamp believes that these individuals have learned to pace their lives. They responded to and appreciated the world around them. They liked simple things like flowers, animals, walks in the park, and the Northern Lights, and they were able to enjoy the traffic along a detour instead of cussing the highway department.

Job: Blessing or Barrier?

Our jobs, of course, demand our time and attention. Some men feel their jobs are too demanding and take them away from other activities. In this new century, more men, especially young men, are speaking up and saying their job is demanding more time and energy than should be either expected or provided. Millennials are those born in the 1980s and 1990s who are demonstrating that they want to live a more balanced life. This generation of Americans will hold most of the jobs in just a few years. But even now I don't believe men can make much of a case to blame their jobs for their lack of close friendships or close family ties. I think that jobs that are extremely demanding and consume most of a man's energy and time are rare these days. And men who do work in these positions usually do so of their own free will.

Ronald Reagan is an example of one who led a balanced life even when saddled with the responsibility of the presidency. Journalist George Will said that Reagan has proven that the presidency is not such a destroyer after all. His immediate predecessor, Jimmy Carter, proudly, even ostentatiously, made the presidency seem crushing. Those who give an inordinate amount of attention to their jobs tend to have few outside interests. While the Bible warns us about the sin of laziness, it also warns us about excessive work, which is unnecessarily demanding. "It is in vain that you rise up early and go late to rest, eating the bread of anxious toil; for he gives to his beloved sleep" (Psalm 127:2 RSV).

We've learned from our culture that our performance in the workplace leads to money, status, and even fame and fortune. Success is not gained from being a loyal friend or a good husband. Rather it comes as a reward for performance on the job. Acquiring and enjoying material wealth is a pursuit worthy of our attention and is justified and defended from such varied sources as the Bible and Adam Smith, author of a book on early capitalist theory in 1776 titled *The Wealth of Nations*. Work gives us pride and satisfaction and a feeling that we are caring for our family and making the world around us a better place. Actor Geoffrey Owens was discovered working at a Trader Joe's grocery store during gaps in his acting career. He was interviewed on *Good Morning America* and eloquently shared with everyone about the dignity of all work. Owens told his boss at Trader Joe's that he hoped he would keep his job open because he might well return to work some more between acting gigs. All work is honorable.

It is true that we can be too busy and too preoccupied. At work, if we're very busy or in some way unavailable, we and others may feel that this busyness translates into being important and responsible. It is usually the man himself who allows himself to become overworked and tends to be the least effective. He finds it difficult to say no to virtually any request. He may feel he must do the task because no one else will complete the task as well as he will.

If you feel you're not a workaholic but that the company is simply demanding more of your time than is justified, it may be reasonable to look for a different, more balanced job. The economic effects of the Great Recession that began in 2008 still linger many years later, and it is therefore not always easy to move from one job to another. The book *What Color Is Your Parachute?* by Richard N. Bolles in the 2019 or later edition is one of many sources that can get you started planning for new employment and a positive career change if you feel that would be appropriate. Another helpful book is Dev Aujla's *50 Ways to Get a Job.*[1]

I was a visiting professor at Roosevelt University the year following the three September 11, 2001, terrorist attacks on America. I was teaching in a department that offered those with college degrees the opportunity to participate in a graduate program where they could complete a master's degree while also acquiring a license to teach within our public schools. We had many nontraditional applicants who were mid-career and successful in well-established businesses. These were individuals who, after the attack upon America on 9/11, sought ways they could give back to their country through perhaps a different career. This was a time when we all came together as Americans. Many students I had at Roosevelt wanted to change course and give back by becoming teachers. It was my privilege and enjoyment to be able to teach several courses with these civic-minded individuals, several of whom changed careers to become K-12 public school teachers.

Some cling to a job they don't like because of pressure or boredom just because it seems secure and they don't want to risk a new employment adventure. If your job truly prevents you from leading a balanced life for whatever reason, you may want to consider a change. Some super-achievers are asking to move to a slower business track at work where they can continue to work hard but without sacrificing parts of a personal life. If, in your judgment, you have invested too many years to change jobs or are locked into a pension plan, perhaps you can change departments or responsibilities without leaving your present employer.

The Real Problem

For most of us, the real problem is not with our jobs but rather with ourselves. It is not our jobs that create the calamity of our friendlessness and even psychosomatic disorders, but rather how we view ourselves and others and how we think and behave that gets us into trouble. We have learned to deny our feelings and keep to ourselves any pain, loneliness, fear, or any other emotion.

A friend from my college days wrote a memoir about his parents' lives together, including their wartime service, she as a registered nurse and he as a B-17 Flying Fortress navigator during the Second World War. My friend Charley writes about their romance during the war and later marriage, family, and careers. Within a section titled Mom's Army Friends, he writes, "As

I remember my parents in their later years, Dad was usually quite reserved, standoffish even. Mom was by far the more extroverted of the two."2

Charley cautions reading too much into his remembrance since his dad learned early that it was emotionally risky to form friendships during the war, especially as an Army Air Force navigator on B-17s because it was all too frequent that planes did not return to their bases. Casualty rates were high. Maybe learning that it was easier to remain strangers left an impression that lasted a lifetime.

I share this story because it is very common for men from Charley's dad's generation not to share many emotions. Journalist Tom Brokaw wrote *The Greatest Generation*, a popular book about this great generation of American men and women who lived and served at home and overseas during the Great Depression and the Second World War.

With many of us men, if we fail to reach some predetermined level of success and accomplishment, this is likely to produce additional frustrations and the sense of being somehow a failure. Someone once said that the birthright of every American male is a chronic sense of personal inadequacy. The problem is not with our failure to reach some artificial standard but possibly rather with the standard itself. An unobtainable dream or standard is the Spanish machismo concept of a man being an unswerving pinnacle of strength. He is the non-emotional creature who surmounts all tasks and problems with unfaltering success.

If we repress our emotions, do they disappear? Denial and repression force our emotions to be revealed in often distorted fashion, either mentally or physically. Every man has a basic need for emotional release. We're unable to survive without it. James Wagenvoord once explained that a man is never able to completely suppress his inner self. He can hide it, or rationalize it, or diminish its importance, but he isn't able to banish that self permanently. Of course, the continual struggle between what he wants and what he thinks is required of him makes his emotions erupt in fits and starts. A brief explosion of inexplicable tears, an outburst of sudden affection, a late-night confidence—these are the humanizing cracks in his mask.

Men seem to falter in their relationships with others partially because they mentally live in a world that no longer exists. For hundreds of years, and in most cultures, human needs were largely material. The main concern was physically survival. Acquiring the basic material necessities of life was a full-time task. Men had little time to do anything but work hard. This emphasis upon survival, however, was altered for most men living in the Western world following the widespread effects of the Industrial Revolution in the mid-eighteenth century. With advances in farming and science, the average working man, regardless of his social class, got to spend fewer hours acquiring the food, shelter, and protection essentials for biological survival.

But technology changes faster than human attitudes and behavior. People may resist change or, without much thought, follow old, outmoded patterns of behavior. Many resist positive change with the exhortation, "But we've never done it that way before." A computer sales guy once told me that people embrace new technology until about the age of forty-five, when they begin to resist new technology. That could be true for some, but I know many who are older who love the new developments in technology.

Despite the removal of the threat of widespread hunger or starvation in Western nations, many among our species still concentrate much of their energy acquiring material wealth as if somehow their very physical survival depends on it. It's been said we are the only species that eats when we are not hungry, drinks when we are not thirsty, and talks when we have nothing to say. Too much attention is devoted to physical concerns at the expense of emotional and spiritual needs. Just as survival needs must be satisfied, so must our emotional and spiritual needs. If neglected or denied, as is the case with many American men, we will witness distorted personalities.

Abraham H. Maslow, the psychologist who advanced our understanding of human motivation, argued that once basic physical needs are met, we are then free to concern ourselves with deeper, more advanced levels of human needs. Maslow contended that the physiological needs of food, water, and air are of obvious and utmost importance. Once these are satisfied, we are then motivated to free ourselves from physical threat or dangers, and to obtain a secure physical environment.

But even with a safe and secure physical and material world well assured, many men continue to work as if the wolf were still at the door. The "how to succeed" books rarely emphasize that the same qualities that take you to the top can also drop you to the bottom. Personality traits don't exist in a vacuum. A virtue in one situation or time period may well be a detriment in another. Holding in high esteem the values of power, materialism, and status may have served men better in years gone by than today. Achieving bodily comforts and positions of power and prestige do not in themselves satisfy the longings of the human heart.

The famous Menninger Clinic, founded in 1919 in Topeka, Kansas, and moved to Houston in 2012, provides a do-it-yourself psychological health checkup for men to evaluate if problems exist in their lives. Here are some of the checkup questions you can consider:

1. What are my goals in life and how realistic are they?
2. Is my use of time and energy helping me to reach these goals?
3. Do I have a proper sense of responsibility, or do I try to do too much and fail to acknowledge my limitations?
4. How do I react to disappointments and losses?
5. How am I coping with stress and anxiety?

6. What is the consistency and. quality of my personal relationships? Are my contacts with others superficial, meager, and unrewarding?
7. From whom do I receive and to whom do I give emotional support? Do I avoid getting support from others for fear of appearing weak?
8. What is the role of love in my life? How much time do I give to listen to and care for others?

Most useful to us I think are questions 6, 7, and 8. Answers to these questions alone should give you some idea about the quality of interpersonal relationships you have with others. Most men do not score very well with the last three questions. Our interpersonal relationships tend to be anemic. When we admit to ourselves that our relationships with others are not what they should be, then we can begin to make positive changes.

To free ourselves from the disruptive social and psychological constraints which we have learned, we need to clearly appreciate our fundamental God-given basic needs. We will turn our attention to this important issue in the next chapter.

Discussion Questions

1. How is a strong network of family and friendships essential to both the quality and quantity of life?

2. How have we as men valued self-reliance to a distorted extreme? How can you change this situation in your own life?

3. Do your behavior and attitudes actually affect both the quality and the length of your life?

4. After you take the do-it-yourself Menninger mental health checkup, discuss the list and your responses with another person or small group. How can you make changes in your life to increase your well-being?

5. Those who lack close relationships are less happy than those who have close friends. How is loneliness a health hazard?

CHAPTER 4

Basic Survival Needs

The LORD will guide you always; he will satisfy your needs....
—Isaiah 58:11

As we grow up, we realize it is less important to have lots of friends and more important to have real friends.
—Amanda McRae

The lyric in an old song Barbra Streisand continues to sing concludes that *people who need people are the luckiest people in the world*. Actually, people who need people are the only people in the world. Not everyone is willing to admit it, but each of us needs intimacy with and the nurture of at least a couple of significant other people in our lives. Even to ourselves we don't often acknowledge the depth of our need for human intimacy.

We are more similar than we are different, but we usually focus our attention upon the differences. It is our human similarities that unite us. Everything I need, you need too. To define what it means to be human is to list the basic emotional needs we have in common within the human family.

There are six basic needs that are common to all humans in all periods of history and across all cultures, age levels, and social classes. They are universal. If these needs are not satisfied, we can suffer from social dysfunction and emotional and spiritual distress.

Just what are our basic emotional soul needs? Psychologists, sociologists, historians, anthropologists, and theologians have, of course, studied this question for time immemorial. In the early part of the last century, sociologist William Thomas worked on this question, as have Louis Raths, Anna Burrell, and other more recent scientists. Their findings are similar. All humans have six specific major emotional needs that must be satisfied if they are to function as well-adjusted individuals. The person who has these six core needs satisfied usually is at peace within and is a contributing member of the society. To reach a positive state of mind and emotion, a person must possess the following in ample supply. I've listed each here with some thoughts I'd like to share with you.

Belonging and Love

Each of us needs to be an important part of some whole. Many suffer from an enormous fear of falling short and being rejected. The need for belonging is the need to feel worthwhile. Having the knowledge that we are accepted and even loved by others provides us with emotional security. Whether we admit it or not, we also need to belong to and be accepted by God. The ultimate fulfillment of belonging is knowing that we are created by God, who loves us. We have worth and dignity not because of what we can do or produce but because we are created beings of Almighty God.

Several decades ago a study was conducted within a South American orphanage. Normal physical care was provided for the babies, but because the orphanage was so badly understaffed, the overworked nurses were largely unable to play with or show much affection to the children. The babies responded at first by crying. Later they lost their appetites and became restless and nervous. More than ninety babies became ill or even died, likely due to a lack of consistent attention and love. Approximately twenty children who survived suffered emotionally as they grew older.

In January 1978, a memorial service was conducted in the U.S. Capitol Rotunda for Hubert Humphrey. Washington's elite gathered to say good-bye to the highly regarded former Minnesota senator, vice president, and presidential candidate. Richard Nixon, who a few years earlier had resigned the presidency over the Watergate scandal, was present that day. This was Nixon's first public appearance since his resignation, and he was off to the side by himself, standing alone as if somehow he was quarantined.

Howard Baker, Republican Senator from Tennessee, remembering that day, said, "Nobody would talk to him. Everybody was afraid of him." The awkward ostracism of the former president ended only when President Jimmy Carter walked over to Mr. Nixon, shook his hand, and welcomed him back to Washington. *Newsweek* magazine concluded that this simple act of humanity and compassion actually changed Nixon's sense of self and his future.

Benjamin and Ruth Lippsett met in the 1920s and were married for sixty-two years. They both died in Santa Fe, New Mexico, within an actual hour of each other. The cause of each death was recorded as heart failure. Benjamin was eighty-nine and Ruth was eighty-six on the day they died. Their daughter, Betty Ann Rose, gave testimony to their wonderful life together. Benjamin adored his wife from the first time he laid eyes on her, right up to the last time he laid eyes on her. The cause of death is listed as heart failure, but that is not what they died from. "He stayed until he knew she was gone and didn't need him anymore. That's the way they wanted it. We told Dad that Mom had gone. He saw her; then he laid down, cried some tears, and within the hour he stopped breathing."

Ronald and Mary Lou McCurdy loved each other and did everything together. They even worked together at Wheaton

College in suburban Chicago. They loved each other but had life struggles, including the deaths of two of their children, in their sixty-three years of marriage. They died within ten days of each other in 2014. Their daughter said, "Dad held on so he could help Mom go through this. Despite multiple health issues they both willed themselves to stick around for each other."

In December 2017, in Medinah, Illinois, after seventy years of marriage, World War II veteran and twice Purple Heart recipient Bob Kretschmer died fifteen minutes after his wonderful wife, Ruth. Their daughter Bobbi said, "Dad hung in there for her. They worked it out between them, through the grace of God." Some call it the "widower effect," when "long married couples so much in love pass away within a short time of each other."

George H.W. Bush, our forty-first president and lifelong public servant, died just a few months after his beloved Barbara passed away. Their good marriage extended for seventy-three years. They married at the end of World War II in 1945, and both passed away in 2018. In a way, they left this world for heaven together, leaving for us such a good example for how to love and how to serve each other and family and friends, and all those whose lives they touched along the way.

Army chaplain and theologian Paul Tillich might not have had marriages like that of the Lippsetts, McCurdys, Kretschmers, and Bushes in mind when he wrote that "there is no life where there is no otherness," but his words came to mind when I heard these stories. In two independent studies, one a nine-year study at the University of California at Berkeley and the other at the University of Michigan, researchers found that adults who are not married or don't belong to nurturing groups or relationships have a death rate much higher than those who have frequent caring human contact.

Last August, Sue Ann and I received a Happy Anniversary card from a couple who are close neighbors. There was a personal note inside, which read, *Dear David and Sue Ann. May you always listen to each other with your hearts, treat each other's feelings like your own, and take time to see the beauty in life and each other. Friends Forever, your neighbors Norman and Juanita.* This note brings a smile and good thoughts. We have their note in a permanent place in our kitchen. Norm and Juanita celebrated their seventieth wedding anniversary on July 3 last year. They are a wonderful couple and so much in love. It's our privilege to have them as neighbors and friends.

Social isolation is at least as significant to mortality rates as smoking, high blood pressure, high cholesterol, obesity, and lack of physical exercise. People cut off from spouses and friends by death or distance or a broken relationship, run a great risk of developing health problems and dying prematurely. We need to belong. Being lonely is hazardous to our health.

While I was in college, my grandmother-in-law broke her hip and was hospitalized for several weeks. On the days my wife or I visited with her, the nurses reported that she was alert and happy for the entire day. But if no one visited her in a twenty-four-hour period, she developed a confused and disoriented persona. It wasn't a lack of human interaction that affected her so dramatically, since many employees entered her room briefly with food and medication.

What was missing on those days we were not with her was the awareness of being with family members who deeply loved her. *We* were what or who was missing. From recent research, we now know that even regularly eating alone can increase your risk of obesity, malnutrition, depression, and even early death. We need to join community groups and meet regularly for breakfast, lunch, or dinner dates with friends and family.

I agree with Daniel Callahan, who wrote years ago in his book *Setting Limits*, that the place of the elderly in a good society is inherently communal, not one that is solely individual. None of us can function well while lacking social and spiritual intimacy with others. We need the love and affection of other people throughout every stage of life.

Accomplishment

Goals, both short-term and long-term, are important to our emotional health. People who feel they are not accomplishing all they should in life usually think of themselves as failures. It's usually enjoyable and rewarding to work toward the successful conclusion of projects and activities large and small.

One of the secrets of longevity is to continue to plan and anticipate. A common trait of those who live in good health to a ripe old age is the desire to live for tomorrow. In Maslow's theory, the accomplishment need is referred to as "self-actualization," or the ongoing desire to improve.

Each of us has a basic need to create, to express ourselves, and to use our talents, even if no one acknowledges our efforts. I heard a story about an elderly Eskimo man who lived in the Alaskan wilderness with only goats, ducks, and chickens for company. When he wasn't either searching for or growing food, he spent his time creating beautiful oil paintings of the majestic scenery that surrounded him. These paintings hung on his cabin wall. He did not need an audience. There was satisfaction simply in the creation of the work, but I do feel there would be even more satisfaction if there were others nearby to share with what was created.

In 1989 the San Francisco area suffered an earthquake that left behind widespread destruction. The majestic Golden Gate Bridge, however, escaped damage. It didn't even buckle. The day after the earthquake, it was reopened for traffic. In more recent earthquakes, including the one in 2013, the Golden Gate Bridge has continued to escape damage. Dr. Charles A. Ellis, an obscure Purdue University professor, was responsible for the engineering design of this magnificent bridge. When it was built during the 1930s and 1940s, Ellis received little notice for his remarkable engineering contribution. Instead, another engineer, Joseph Strauss, received the public's acclaim because he was more visible as a promoter and fund-raiser of the construction project.

For his efforts, a statue of Strauss sits at the foot of the bridge, but no such monument was erected in Dr. Ellis' honor. Ellis was never troubled by the absence of attention. He believed that self- and public acclamation was unimportant. "What really matters," he said, "are the accomplishments we leave behind to the benefit of others."

This is very true, but if we have an opportunity to share the results of some accomplishments with loved ones or friends that we are proud of, it can be very satisfying. When you have received a trophy for some athletic or public service accomplishment, did you put it under your bed and store it out of sight of family and friends? My guess is that you displayed it and enjoyed telling others close to you about your accomplishments. Trophies, like any expression of our talents, are for sharing with people whom we care about and who care about us.

Meaning and Purpose

We need a sense of accomplishment, but we need something more and beyond what accomplishment alone can provide. Harold Kushner, in his book *When All You've Ever Wanted Isn't Enough*, states that our lives may be successful or unsuccessful, full of glory or full of worry, but do they mean anything?[1] The famous Swiss psychologist Carl Jung observed from his years of practice that many of his patients were not clinically ill or neurotic but suffered from an emptiness and a lack of meaning. According to Jung, "The central neurosis of our time is emptiness." In the play *Death of a Salesman*, the character Willy Loman examines his many lonely years of existence and concludes that life is meaningless. Such despair we can thankfully avoid with a heartfelt and prayerful search for God's plan and purpose for our lives.

The Westminster Shorter Catechism, first published in 1647, records that "Man's chief end is to glorify God and enjoy Him forever." It is God who made us, and we are His. That's what the psalmist tells us in Psalm 100:3. It is God who gives meaning to our lives. I need to remind myself sometimes that God is God and I am not.

When we know what we are supposed to do with our lives and are willing to work hard, we then have a sense of well-being and satisfaction from accomplishing something meaningful and worthwhile. Meeting this basic need provides significance in our life. Many people are able to meet this need with employment, volunteer activity at church, or some form of public service. We need to feel that what we do in life is important and has meaning and purpose.

In his book Man's Search for Meaning, Victor Frankl writes just after the end of World War II about the emotions and behavior of human beings under the most horrific circumstances, and shares lessons for spiritual and physical survival.2 Millions of innocent civilians were forced into Nazi concentration death camps. Not everyone arrested under the Nazis' barbaric regime was sent to the gas chambers. Some languished in camps under unspeakable conditions. In the ghastly environment of concentration camps, Frankl noted that while some gave up and soon died, others persisted, clinging to life despite the horrific outward circumstances.

Frankl found the survivors usually had several things in common that sustained their will to live. The survivors had a purpose for living. Life had meaning. There were loved ones somewhere they desperately wanted to see again. They did not succumb to the desperation that they had been abandoned by either God or people they loved. These individuals had a responsibility to others. Life was more than just about themselves. They were needed, and they had a future they longed for and anticipated.

Harold Kushner's findings agree with Frankl's. Concerning innocent civilians in Hitler's death camps, Kushner concludes, "Those prisoners whose sense of self depended mainly upon their wealth, their social position, and their prestigious jobs tended to fall apart when those things were taken from them. The prisoners whose sense of self grew out of their religious faith or their own self-esteem, rather than other people's opinions of them, tended to function better."3

Joy often comes to our lives when we have three integral ingredients: 1) something to do, 2) someone to love, and 3) something to hope for. When you have something important to do, someone to love, along with hopes and dreams for the future, you are better prepared to enjoy the present and anticipate the future. "Those who have a 'why' for living can better handle the 'whats,'" said philosopher Friedrich Nietzsche. Life must have meaning and purpose.

Freedom from Obsessive Fear and Guilt

Regret about how we occasionally behave and think is normal. We usually know when we do something stupid. Dr. Karl Menninger, in his thoughtful book *Whatever Became of Sin?*, argued that we need certain forms of fear and guilt to help motivate us to be responsible and to do what is right. Very true but negative, obsessive, unconscious fears can undermine our happiness and affect our personality and contribute to making us act weirdly. Irrational fears can distort reality and destroy our capacity to deal effectively with the outside world.

A woman who worked in a real estate office on the north side of Chicago was always fearful of what other people thought. She selected her clothes, chose her words, and behaved on the basis of what she thought was acceptable to others, both friends and strangers alike. When I taught psychology classes, I would refer to this type of condition as the "dictatorship of the they." This woman and millions like her are crippled with concerns about what the often-nebulous "they" might think instead of living in harmony with their own well-established, spiritual, social, and emotional values.

Such people can be unsure of their own worth. What is needed is freedom from their fears and guilt. This freedom frequently comes through hard emotional work, requiring a break from the shackles of old perceptions and the grasping of new vistas that can contribute to a satisfying and enjoyable life.

Self-Respect

Self-confidence and self-respect are prerequisites for a constructive and purposeful life. Our feelings about ourselves are developed during our interactions and relationships with other people.

A college student was home for Christmas vacation. He told his mother he needed to spend time with his father. Father and son went to the family room and talked for more than two hours. Alone they talked about life, love, careers, grades, and the future. Later the mother asked, "What did he want?" The father proudly responded, "Me."

Striving to feel good about yourself is not self-preoccupation or narcissism. You need to feel good about yourself or you'll be less able to do good and positive things. The biblical admonition to "love your neighbor as yourself" (Mark 12:31) is built upon this reality. John Powell, author of *The Secret of Staying in Love*, argues that all psychological problems, from a mild neurosis to the deepest psychosis, are symptomatic of the frustration of this fundamental human need for a healthy sense of self-respect. When we possess self-confidence, we are equipped to get our minds off of ourselves and then focus upon the needs of those who may need our attention.

Understanding

The basic human need of understanding has two sides. Each individual needs to have his attitudes, beliefs, and ideas understood by others. We need people in our lives who really understand us. Conversely, we need to experience and understand deeply the attitudes and feelings of others. To accomplish this interaction requires in-depth communication in which empathy is expressed. When issues that really matter are actually talked about, then there is potential for life-changing fellowship. Psychologist Larry Crabb suggests that in good relationships, we actually have a responsibility to give feedback lovingly and to receive feedback non-defensively.

Part of understanding is being open and responsible to and with a few trusted friends. We can be accountable to a few men whom we might be close to, if we are open. They can help us see our blind spots, which can sometimes send us in the wrong direction. This is the meaning from Proverbs 27:17, which states, "As iron sharpens iron so one man sharpens another." There may be occasional friction and tension when men choose to be accountable with each other, but this is where life is to be lived at its best. In an attempt at humor one guy says to his friend, "We'll always be best friends—because you know too much." Many of us are tempted to do life on our own. And men on their own tend to do wasteful and even self-destructive things. We can tolerate stress and live lives much better when a precious few individuals understand our struggles and we understand their challenges.

As we conclude this chapter, I want to emphasize that meeting our basic needs is a prerequisite for leading a normal spiritual and socially bountiful life. And to want these six basic needs satisfied is no more selfish than to want food and water for your body or spiritual food for your soul.

Discussion Questions

1. Why do we often focus upon our differences when there are many human similarities that could unite us?

2. One of our most profound needs is for social and spiritual intimacy. How can friendships meet this need in the areas of giving and receiving?

3. How does our self-respect, the way we feel about ourselves, contribute to our ability to form successful relationships with others?

CHAPTER 5

What's the Difference?

Male and female He created them.
—Genesis 1:27

Why can't a woman be more like a man?
—From My Fair Lady, lyrics by Alan Jay Lerner

Women are different from men. God deliberately created both male and female. John Gray's book *Men Are from Mars, Women Are From Venus* originally got a lot of attention in the 1990s and continues to do so yet today.[1] It's obvious to all of us that men and women are different, even though we are from the same planet. Both the men and the women I interviewed agreed that women make friends more easily than men. They form and sustain relationships at a more qualitative level than do men. From the interviews I conducted, I've concluded that friendship means more and is different to women than it is to men. Their relationships tend to be more meaningful, more satisfying, and of longer duration.

These two assumptions, that the sexes differ and that women have more satisfying friendships than men, are widely held beliefs that require little validation. But here the agreement ends. The difficult questions we need to deal with are: How do the sexes differ? Does maleness or femaleness affect the making and nurturing of relationships with other humans? Do the differences affect our ability to form friendships? Can we as men blame sex differences for our being generally friendless? Must maleness somehow hinder a man from forming and sustaining close relationships with other men? The explorations of these questions should help us better understand both our limitations and our potential as men with regard to friendships.

Sexual differences are facts of nature. Many are too obvious to even mention. Much of the research dealing with the sexes has been conducted in an attempt to demonstrate that females are equal in all areas to males. Therefore, there has been a distinct tendency to devote little attention to the differences that do exist. Understanding some of the differences should be useful as we learn more about friendships. Let's look at a few of the wonderful differences between the sexes.

Physical Differences

Despite the claims of some people, the sexes really are different. In a survey of the literature on sex differences, it is not difficult to find dozens of studies that show that significant differences do indeed exist between men and women. These differences are not just limited to sex organs. For example, in all human societies men are larger and stronger than women. The average man is 6 percent taller than the average woman. Also, men average about 20 percent more weight than women. The greater body bulk of the male comes mainly from larger muscles and bones. Large muscles in males permit them to lift more weight, throw a ball farther, or run faster than most women. Even at birth, the male has more strength to lift his head higher and for longer periods of time than does a female. At puberty, the difference in muscle strength is accentuated, largely due to the male hormone testosterone.

Men have a higher metabolic rate and produce more physical energy than women, and they appear to need more food to keep the body performing at its full potential. Men's blood is slightly different from women's, with an average of 300,000 more red corpuscles per cubic millimeter.

With statistics like these, it's understandable that many have concluded that men are physically superior to women. Even some scientists who should know better have fallen for the male biological superiority fallacy. Not too surprisingly, just about all of these scientists have been men. For example, Lester Ward, a founding father of American sociology, stated that women were cautious and more conservative than men because of their biological deficiencies. Contemporary sociologists and scientists no longer believe or at least no longer talk much about these inaccurate theories. We know now that rather than being physically inferior, women actually possess certain biological advantages when compared with men.

The late Dr. Estelle Ramey, an endocrinologist formerly from Georgetown University School of Medicine, believed that women outlive men because they are biologically stronger, not because they lead lives that are less stressful. Anthropologist Ashley Montagu argued in his book *The Natural Superiority of Women* that women are actually biologically and genetically superior to their male counterparts. Montagu provided many examples of how women live longer and perform better than men because their biological endurance is superior to men.

Biological differences are established at conception. It is estimated that about 130 males are conceived for every 100 females. Conception is probably the male's only fundamental biological advantage. But after the beginning of human life, it's downhill for the male sex. At the time of birth, there are approximately 106 boys to every 100 girls. More male fetuses are miscarried than female fetuses. The United States Bureau of Vital Statistics estimates that 25 percent more boy babies than girl babies are born prematurely. Circulatory and respiratory infection, parasites, and viral and digestive diseases plague boys in higher numbers than girls. In fact, there is rarely a disease or defect that doesn't damage boys more than girls.

During the first year of life, the mortality rate among boys is almost one third higher than among girls. Boys have more genetic defects that contribute to their higher death rate. And as if that were not enough, the female physical advantage goes on throughout life into old age. Men and women differ in every cell of their bodies. In the nucleus of each body's millions of cells, there is present either an XX chromosome for women or an XY chromosome for men. For centuries husbands have placed on their wives the burden of producing a healthy boy baby. And yet the genetic fact is that if a baby is to be a boy, the father must come up with the Y chromosome, which is the primary male gender determiner.

Each female cell contains the chromatin substance that is absent in male cells. The male nervous system, too, is different from a woman's, as are other parts of his body. We are reminded of the biblical truth that God created humans distinctly as male and female: "God created man in His own image; in the image of God He created him; male and female He created them" (Genesis 1:27).

Psychological Differences

If the sexes are different physically, aren't they also different emotionally? Unless we believe that mind and body are completely separate realms, we would suspect that there are emotional differences as well as physical differences between the sexes. As you might imagine, this topic is fraught with controversy and many differences of opinion that will not be resolved in a brief discussion here.

People tend to hold as many different points of view on this psychological and emotional topic as they do on the biological subject. One group claims that men and women are very different emotionally. For example, they say that women are religious, men are not. Women are gentle, men are rough. Men are independent, women are dependent. Women talk a great deal, while men talk very little. Women appreciate the arts and literature, men do not. Women need to care for children, men do not. Men need goals and accomplishments, women do not. And the list of stereotypes goes on and on.

This group maintains that heredity makes men and women completely different, not only physically but also in the way we think and behave. Some of the men who hold this view are chauvinists who have acquired a stereotype of what women are like. Some chauvinists are also playboys who view women as possessions and as sexual objects. The playboy mentality of lust still maintains that the ideal woman has a small brain and large breasts. This was certainly the base and immoral selfish view of *Playboy* founder Hugh Hefner, who spent his entire self-centered, sexual predatory life celebrating promiscuous sex while overtly critical of Christians and marriage fidelity before his death a few years ago.

Some men who don't believe in the playboy's distorted and destructive views nevertheless still hold a chauvinistic view of the sexes. Some books and sermons that deal with family living issues discuss the role of men and women from a chauvinistic perspective. For example, many emphasize that the Bible says wives should "submit" to their husbands (Ephesians 5:22), but they neglect to mention that the Scripture also records that husbands and wives are admonished to submit themselves to each other. In the verse prior to the frequently cited Ephesians 5:22, we find, "Submit to one another out of reverence for Christ" (Ephesians 5:21). Submission is not for wives only.

To submit is to pay less attention to yourself and more to the needs of your spouse. Biblical submission is the putting aside of your own rights so you can better serve the one you love. Submission implies a conciliatory mind-set. Submission is not an act of blind obedience but rather an expressed concern for your spouse even at the expense of your own personal desires. Submission is not exclusively a male or female thing. It is rather a biblical and human principle about relationships. We don't hear this very much, even in church, because we are locked in a culture that does not view submission as a desirable trait for either men or women.

There is another extreme way of thinking that contends that there really are no psychological, emotional, or mental differences between the sexes. Men and women are said to have the same abilities to perform or behave in exactly the same fashion if given the same chances and the same early educational experiences. This approach maintains that all differences are culturally determined and have nothing to do with gender. Those of this persuasion say that the typical woman acts like she does because she was taught to act in a certain fashion by parents, teachers, and society.

In the 1930s, the well-known anthropologist Dr. Margaret Mead studied the differences in male and female behavior in three tribes of New Guinea. She argued that sex roles are different in different areas of the world and thus concluded that we have no basis for linking one's biological gender with one's behavior or attitude.

I had an opportunity to talk with Dr. Mead about the topic of sex differences during a national anthropology conference many years ago in Chicago. Our conversation took place only a few months before she died. She seemed to have changed her published views somewhat when we talked, or at least held them with less intensity. Dr. Mead seemed to doubt some of her earlier held conclusions, believing now that there might exist innate emotional differences between the sexes, but she was unwilling to speculate specifically on which traits might be either learned or innate.

What Is Male? What Is Female?

Both views of the psychological traits of the sexes—that they are completely innate or that they are totally learned—are largely distortions found at opposite ends of a spectrum. Both of these positions do little to advance our understanding. There really are differences, but they are not as extensive as some would like us to believe. There is substantial evidence that men and women exhibit similar behavior and, in some areas, manifest different behavior. Widespread agreement exists among anthropologists, psychologists, and theologians alike.

From all the hundreds of possible behaviors, only a handful seem to be plainly either mainly male or mainly female. Only a few years ago, few would have foreseen women serving our country on military frontlines, in corporate leadership, and as elected officials. Some of the few differences that likely do exist as innate include that women are more likely than men to express their emotions and display empathy and compassion more than men in response to the emotions of others.

Men and boys as a whole are more skillful than women and girls at visually perceiving the spatial, or geometric, features of objects. Girls score higher than boys on tests of verbal ability, such as comprehension and production of language, analogies, and spelling. Boys achieve slightly higher mathematical scores than girls. This may be a result of boys' superior visual/spatial ability, a capacity useful in solving some mathematical problems. Boys tend to be more physically active than girls, doing more running and jumping. But boys seem not to be using their aptitudes to focus in school. Boys spend more time than girls playing video games and trawling the internet. Unlike years ago, boys are being outclassed by girls in the classrooms of our K-12 schools and universities. I guess that some perceive that for boys it's not cool to do well in school, as it's not particularly cool for boys to be smart.

Aside from these few differences and even some of these that may be partially determined by culture, I believe that few God-ordained differences exist between the sexes. Therefore, there is nothing stopping men from acquiring positive traits and behaviors that will lead to more satisfying relationships with both women and men. Yes, women are more likely than men to express emotions and reveal empathy and compassion, but it seems that nothing exists in either Scripture or biology that says that even if women do these things better than men, men can't improve. Men can learn these traits too.

We're capable of more diverse behavior than we might realize. For example, cleaning dishes may, in the minds of some, be viewed as a woman's or a child's domestic chore, but this idea comes from our culture, certainly not from the Bible. In fact, 2 Kings 21:13 in the King James Version of Scripture mentions a man wiping dishes. My wife originally brought this interesting verse to my attention. Sue Ann is a better cook than I am, so I work at helping out in the kitchen. We agree that these and several other domestic activities are not gender-determined.

Certain domestic tasks in our society, such as changing diapers, mowing the lawn, grocery shopping, driving the kids to school, managing the checkbook, and housecleaning, are still referred to by some to be either a woman's work or a man's work. This role fixation is cultural rather than biologically determined or biblically based. When I worked with the international accreditation of private schools in Saudi Arabia and Egypt, I discovered that only the men in Saudi Arabia, who were usually the fathers, were allowed to pick up children from school. In American schools, usually the mothers drop off and pick up children from school. The Saudi women in 2018 were finally allowed to drive cars and now are allowed to pick up sons and daughters from school.

My wife and I, and our children when they were younger, would do the housecleaning together. Sometimes we called this activity "dummy time," I guess because no one really wants to do it. But working together can be fun or at least tolerable, and the time so spent is over much sooner when more than one person works at it. Today we sometimes get our grandkids involved picking up their toys, puzzles, and books while singing a cleanup song. Sometimes this approach works and sometimes it doesn't. Family members can just pick any job to do when work needs to be done instead of wasting time trying to decide which job is for males and which is for females. Just do the different jobs and be done with it.

One man, following his wife's request that he help with the housework, remarked sarcastically, "That's not my job. The next thing I know you'll be asking me to wear dresses and use perfume and makeup." Actually, we can find historical illustrations when wigs, bloomers, long stockings, lace blouses, and high heels were worn by men and considered manly in the time period in which they appeared. It's difficult to believe, but during America's colonial period, many of these items were popular with some men. Sue Ann and I, with our friends Gary and Jayne Smit, were in London when we all witnessed barristers deliberating in an ornate courtroom before a panel of judges. The barristers in law were all men and all were donning white wigs and robes. The barristers and the judges were all very dignified.

Different cultures and different times of history define manliness differently. What it means to be masculine can be socially as well as biologically determined. True strength of character always reveals itself in gentleness and courtesy. This was the whole medieval concept of knighthood and chivalry. We tend to confuse rudeness with power and aggressiveness with virility. Our definition of manliness or masculinity can be narrow and distorted. We see men and women as opposites. We even use the phrase "the opposite sex," but we're not opposite and we're not from different planets. We are, however, different and how grateful we are for that. Remember, of the forty-eight chromosomes in each human cell, only one relates specifically to gender.

The Biblical Perspective

Throughout history, most people have assumed that a proper interpretation of Genesis 1:27 including, "...male and female he created them" meant that any and all differences in their society between males and females existed because God created these differences.

In recent generations, we have begun to question the "absolute role" that biology plays in the formation of sexual temperament and behavior. Culture and nature together are the principal influences determining the temperamental differences between the sexes. We are more alike than we previously realized. Women began in large numbers to enter the workforce during World War II when most able-bodied men were in the armed services.

Women entered nearly every kind of job and industry as part of the war effort. There were patriotic posters featuring Rosie the Riveter helping to win the war effort on the home front. After the war, many women remained in the workforce, and now the majority of women are working outside the home. Men today are more likely to help with children and with domestic tasks that historically have been considered a woman's work. Gone are the 1950s *The Adventures of Ozzie and Harriet* and *Leave It to Beaver* and *Father Knows Best* television stereotypes, when the husband was the sole provider and his wife was the home-based spouse who cared for the kids and prepared meals.

Those with a faith-based orientation may assume that the particular definition of masculinity and femininity learned in our culture is God's definition. During our youth we can easily absorb an ethnocentric view of the world. We fall into this trap by reading and projecting our cultural expectations into Scripture. But we don't know some things for sure, so it's alright to ponder in some areas what is true and what God might have in mind. There will always be times when we don't know for sure. This may be part of the message we find in 1 Corinthians 13:1 (KJV), where we read, "For now we see through a glass darkly." The NIV translates this verse as: "Now we see but a poor reflection as in a mirror."

When the Bible comments on basic human traits, it doesn't distinguish between the sexes. In the Sermon on the Mount (Matthew 5), the Lord calls those blessed who are sorrowful, who possess a gentle spirit, who show mercy, whose hearts are pure, and who are peaceful. The same is true of the spiritual gifts listed in 1 Corinthians 12. The apostle Paul did not list any gifts with gender tags. Wow. We are more alike than we are different. This is good news! You are more malleable than you might have realized. Sure, you're a man, but that doesn't mean you can't learn to be a compassionate, courteous, loving, listening, caring human being if you're presently lacking or possess in modest amounts any of these or other positive characteristics.

If you don't now have the traits for developing friendships, you can definitely acquire them. You can ask yourself whether some aspect of your personality is a positive attribute or whether it is destructive. If a certain behavior hinders the formation of friendships, it can be viewed not so much as masculine but rather as destructive. If behavior encourages friendship formation, view this behavior as positive, not just uniquely feminine.

The great thing about learned negative behavior is that you can unlearn it and thus gain a fresh start. For years, a woman cut off both ends of a ham before cooking it. Her inquisitive young daughter asked, "Why do you cut off each end, Mom?" The response: "I don't really know. I've always done it that way. I guess I learned it from your grandmother." Undaunted, the little girl next asked her grandmother why both she and Mother "cut off the ends." Grandmother was surprised to learn that this had become a family tradition. "Honey," she said, "I had to cut off the ends because most hams wouldn't fit well in my small roasting pan."

This is a humorous story, but it is one with a message. We have learned many things in life, and what we have learned contributes to the way we currently live our lives. Some of what we have learned, like the lady who still hacks off the ends of the ham, is unnecessary but harmless. We have also acquired, from earlier learning, much that is positive and good. But some aspects of our early socialization consist of cultural baggage that we could dispose of.

Being a man need not be a social handicap and should not be used by us to defend a lonely existence. A man I interviewed told me, "Of course I don't have friends. I'm a man. My wife is the one with the friends." His implication was that his friendless condition was part of his genetic code rather than just his social upbringing. Our biological maleness need not be a barrier to developing relationships, and social barriers can be dismantled.

It's been said that we are all self-made, but it seems only the rich and successful admit it. If we are not happy with our situation, we can change. Only our resistance to change prevents us from cultivating the warm, meaningful relationships enjoyed by most women and just a few men.

Discussion Questions

1. Do you believe that being a man should in any way affect your ability to form quality friendships? Why? Why not?

2. In what ways has our culture provided definitions of what it means to be male that is in conflict with the Bible?

3. We use the term "opposite sex." Are there other terms that may be more appropriate?

4. What aspects of your personality that may be harmful can you change? How might accountable fellowship with other men, and personal commitments and prayer make a difference?

CHAPTER 6

Biblical Principles of Friendship

You have made known to me the path of life.
—Psalm 16:11

There's no life where there's no otherness.
—Paul Tillich

I t's not as easy as you might think to recognize the true nature of friendship. What's referred to as friendship might
not really be friendship. It's easy to mistake it for one of
various counterfeits. Fortunately, the Bible offers examples and
principles of friendship for us to learn and use in our own lives.

For a biblical example of what not to do in a friendship, we
can turn to what is probably the oldest book in the Bible—Job.
This great section of Scripture illustrates that, despite very difficult circumstances, we nevertheless really do have the capacity
for a faith completely centered on God.

Job lost his health, his children, and much that he owned.
He lost the support of his friends, and his wife was impatient
with his tragic circumstances, advising him to "Curse God and
die!" (Job 2:9). Job's multiple sufferings were compounded not
just with a lack of sympathy but with overt emotional harassment and condemnation by his three so-called friends, Zophar,
Eliphaz, and Bildad. They told Job he must have committed some
gross sin for all these calamities to befall him. Why else would
he be suffering?

Eliphaz summed up their thinking when he asked Job a rhetorical question: "Remember now, whoever perished being innocent? Or where were the upright ever cut off?" Eliphaz continued without waiting for Job's response: "Even as I have seen, those who plow iniquity and sow trouble reap the same" (Job 4:7–8). You can almost hear the judgmental and self-righteous tone in the voices of these guys as you read the passage. The fact is, these pseudo friends, with their criticism and self-righteousness, failed to look at Job's pain from a different perspective. They reached the easy but wrong conclusion that God must be punishing Job for some unrevealed hidden sin.

If we had to choose a friendship like that between David and Jonathan or that of Job and his three friends, we would all prefer the kindness and commitment that existed between David and Jonathan. But close friendships don't just happen. They result from the application of principles recorded throughout the Bible.

While preparing to write this book along with conducting surveys, I read through the Bible with the goal of finding principles for friendship. I was at first surprised to learn that the Bible has so much to say about this important topic. We tend to think of the Bible as a book of God's grace and personal redemption, which it surely is, but the Bible also includes a great deal about our relationships with other people. In fact, the Bible touches upon virtually every kind of human relationship, including friendship.

The Bible places emphasis upon six principles of friendship. These basic themes keep appearing in different examples throughout Scripture. In the following discussion of these six principles, we can explore which traits need more of our individual attention and perhaps better application in our personal lives.

Principle 1: Worldview Centered upon God
The Westminster Shorter Catechism from the seventeenth century, mentioned earlier, recorded that "Man's chief end is to

glorify God and to enjoy Him forever." Intimate friendships rarely develop when individuals do not share at least a basic consensus of beliefs. In Psalm 1:1 we read that "blessed is the man who walks not in the counsel of the ungodly." Second Corinthians 6:14 states, "Do not be unequally yoked together with unbelievers." Two men with the same biblical value system can seek each other's counsel with confidence that the responses will be based upon scriptural principles. David went to Jonathan for counsel (1 Samuel 20), knowing the advice would be sound. Moses accepted the advice of Jethro (Exodus 18:13–27), as Timothy did of Paul (1 Timothy 6:11–16; 2 Timothy 3:10–17).

Jerry and his family and my family attended the same church for years in the Chicago area. During a conversation, I remember Jerry saying that "at times I need to let my hair down, tell someone something important to me and maybe about me and enjoy a relationship with another man built on years of trust and confidence." Usually we have this kind of openness mainly with people with whom we share similar values, but this may not always be true.

I have two friends who do not share either my Christian values or political views. John and I were in school together. Our ideas are often different, but we share a respect for each other and will listen to each other's views. I have a similar relationship with my friend Bill. He's more liberal than I am and is turned off by the Christian fundamentalism that he experienced with his parents and siblings. Despite our differences, we have maintained a friendship throughout the years, largely because of a mutual respect. I continue to share my worldview and my Christ-centered faith with these two men, both of whom continue to listen and to consider what I might share. And I will continue to listen to their sharing with me, primarily on political topics. Recently we have talked about the pragmatic reasons for belief in God, presented in Blaise Pascal's Wager. And we've talked also about the grace message provided by God given to us in the Bible in many places, including John 3:16. The friendship I have with John and Bill are good ones that I value, but I think they are rare. Most close friends share similar core values.

Principle 2: Formation of Covenant
"And Jonathan made a covenant with David because he loved him as himself" (1 Samuel 18:3).

Virtually every important relationship or event in our society is acknowledged with ritual and ceremony in the presence of others. Marriage is the most obvious illustration of this. The newly married couple is formally recognized by relatives, friends, the church, and even the legal structure. Recognition marks what anthropologists call "rites of passage." Rites in society occur at birth, baptism, graduation, marriage, club initiations, retirements, and death. These and other transitions are usually accompanied by some formal ritual that signifies the passing from one significant stage of life into another. Through ceremony, we recognize that which we regard with honor.

After an individual has received God's grace by asking Christ to forgive their sins and are "born again," some churches ask for public profession of the conversion experience. In Romans 10:9–10, Paul wrote about the need for a public profession. The congregation witnesses and acknowledges and offers support for the new believer's expression of faith. Congregational support is also proclaimed with the events of baptism and when joining a church. The symbolism of baptism reflects the reality found in Romans 6:3–4, where we read we are buried with Him unto death and raised with Him to live a new life with Christ.

The significant events in our lives are enriched and more memorable when we include ceremony. Despite what many young and some older people think, we do benefit from rituals in our lives. In the musical *Fiddler on the Roof*, the lovable character Tevya sings of his strong belief in rituals and traditions. Traditions can bring joy and meaning and intimacy in families and friendships. We have a need for the formation of commitments which are witnessed by others. They help provide meaning, acceptance of transition, recognition, and encouragement for ourselves and others. Covenants inform those in our world that the commitment we have taken is important.

In America, the important relationship of friendship is largely lacking any type of ceremony and covenant formation. When we decide to commit to a friendship, rarely if ever is there a public testimony or occasion for acknowledgment by family and other friends. A ceremony to acknowledge a new friendship seems odd or somehow strange. We might be uncomfortable with some friendship acknowledgment.

The Bible, however, encourages the establishment of a covenant when men become friends. Jonathan and David, because of their mutual affection, decided to make a covenant. A covenant is a promise, a verbal agreement, a binding agreement, and a formation of unity. "The soul of Jonathan was knit to the soul of David." *Knit*, a term which means "to unite," is the same word used in Genesis to express Jacob's love for his youngest son, Benjamin (Genesis 35:18). To show outwardly his inward love, Jonathan took off his robe, sword, bow, and belt and gave them all to his dear friend David. This symbolic gesture, this outward expression of Jonathan's love, affected greatly their commitment to each other. David, being a peasant and therefore not wealthy, could return "only" the gift of loyalty and respect to his friend.

The giving and accepting of a tangible token to represent commitment helps solidify friendships like the exchanging of rings during a wedding ceremony. Friends can give modest gifts and remember important days and anniversaries with cards, calls, and letters. These expressions of our friendship should be thoughtful, personal, and creative. I still use the pencil sharpener a friend gave me when I entered college so long ago. I still smile when I think of the friend who gave me a red maple tree sapling for my birthday. He knew I wanted more shade in the backyard of our home. At the time it was the thought that mattered, and it didn't seem important that it would likely take fifteen years or more before the "tree" would cast any shade. A few weeks ago, I asked my friend Jerry to meet me for breakfast and conversation. He agreed, and we had a good discussion. I said that part of the reason for meeting was to celebrate his birthday and therefore, this time, I was paying the bill. This, of course, was no big deal, but he seemed to appreciate it.

Modest gifts are appreciated, but it is the giver, the one who thought of us, whom we remember. The commitment of the friend and the covenant between us has been acknowledged by the simple gift. Today I'm sending a birthday greeting to my friend Arnold. Not a big deal but I want to say with the card that "I'm thinking about you, Arnold, and I value our friendship." It is vital that friends know that we care about them. The very least we can do is tell them how we value them and our relationship. These are expressions of our informal covenants with friends.

Principle 3: Faithfulness
There are few things more troubling than someone who is unpredictable and cannot be counted on when you really need him. In Proverbs 14:20 and 19:4, we read that wealth adds many friends. Fair-weather friends may be plentiful, but they are not worth much. The writer of Proverbs says that a true friend "sticks closer than a brother" (18:24), and we are admonished, "Do not forsake your friend" (27:10).

While the world's philosophy tends to be "Laugh and the world laughs with you; cry and you cry alone," biblical friendship calls for faithfulness. Circumstances should not affect our consistency and dependability. In Romans 12:15 (RSV) the Bible encourages us to "rejoice with those who rejoice," and to "weep with those who weep."

Do you remember Job's three friends? I think of them when I read Proverbs 25:19: "Trust in a faithless man in time of trouble is like a bad tooth or a foot that slips" (RSV). This is a rather graphic illustration of the grief one can suffer from an unfaithful friend. Unfaithfulness often rears its ugly head at times when we are most vulnerable. Sickness, divorce, unemployment, depression, or poverty can quickly thin the ranks of "friends."

A popular young man I know went through a painful divorce. I was very surprised, for Carl and his wife seemed to be the "model couple." Carl's wife fell for the attention and charm of her financially successful and handsome boss. Everyone in Carl's close-knit neighborhood was surprised when they learned about the affair. Carl had no inkling of what was going on behind his back and was shocked and devastated. During and following the divorce, he needed the companionship and support of his friends. And yet at this time in his life when he needed them most, some of his friends began to give him somewhat of a cold shoulder. How could this happen?

So much of our social lives is structured in couple-oriented activities. Carl was no longer part of his former neighborhood group of married couples. I think the rejection of friends may have gone deeper. Carl was now an unattached, young, good-looking man who was perceived, not as a lonely, grief-stricken person who needed his neighborhood friends during a difficult period, but rather as a possible threat. The reasoning might have been, "Who knows? Maybe he'll try to get sympathy and emotional support and even affection from my wife." This kind or reasoning could be conscious or subconscious on the part of the men who seemed to abandon their friend Carl when he needed them the most.

Faithfulness is critical to a close relationship because we learn to depend on those who are close to us. Christ's deepest hurts occurred within His circle of closest companions. David was wounded emotionally more by the treachery of his close friends than by the hostile efforts of his enemies. He lamented in Psalm 55:12–14, "If an enemy were insulting me, I could endure it; if a foe were raising himself against me, I could hide from him. But it is you, a man like myself, my companion, my close friend, with whom I once enjoyed sweet fellowship as we walked with the throng at the house of God."

Julius Caesar was likely not surprised about an assassination conspiracy by Roman senators but was shocked and said "Even you, Brutus?" just before he was killed in 44 BC by his "friend" Marcus Brutus. The apostle Paul was left to stand alone. He writes to Timothy about when he was deserted by Demas and others (2 Timothy 4:10). There was a rupture between Paul and Barnabas and also conflict between Peter and Paul. There may be legitimate as well as not so legitimate explanations for disagreements and conflict among men.

A faithful friend keeps confidences. In Proverbs we read that "a perverse man stirs up dissension and a gossip separates close friends" (16:28). And in 17:9, "He who covers over an offense promotes love, but whoever repeats the matter separates close friends." When friendship involves revealing yourself in confidence to another, and thus becoming vulnerable, this is as it should be, and it is what makes betrayal so evil and faithfulness so virtuous.

Principle 4: Social Involvement

In our mobile society, where upward to approximately 20 percent of our population moves annually, some men are not willing to devote time and attention to forming lasting commitments to either a community or to individuals. The thinking of some is, "We don't expect to live here too long, and I need to focus mainly on my work." And yet Scripture admonishes us to be good neighbors, involved in the lives of others. Being good neighbors can be a form of friendship.

A good neighbor or friend is not only reluctant to start trouble (Proverbs 3:29) but also unwilling to spread it (Proverbs 25:8,9). Silence is better than criticism. When I was a boy of ten or eleven, my father told me, "If you can't say something good about somebody, don't say anything at all." My wife, Sue Ann, has told me on more than one occasion that I don't need to say everything that might enter my mind. She is likely to share this admonition just after I've said something less than useful or even stupid. I'm trying to learn to just let some thoughts come and go without being expressed. Maybe they'll go the way they came. Somewhat humorous is the saying that "a wise man once said... nothing." So often when we spread unflattering or even untruthful statements, we really tell others more about our own character than we do about the person we are condemning. In fact, the Bible says that the man who "does not bridle his tongue, deceives his own heart; this one's religion is useless" (James 1:26). This is surely very sobering.

When Jesus was asked by a lawyer, "Who is my neighbor?" the Lord responded with the parable of the good Samaritan. A man was going from Jerusalem to Jericho when he was robbed and beaten. The thieves left him to die. A priest and later a Levite traveled past the victim but refused to get involved. Lacking basic human compassion, these two leaders went by, leaving the man to possibly die.

The next man on the scene was a Samaritan. The Samaritans were the social outcasts of Jesus' day, similar to the untouchables' class of people from India. This man, the Samaritan, cared for the victim's wounds and took him to a local boardinghouse to recuperate. He paid an innkeeper for the night and promised to pay all the victim's expenses until he was well enough to travel. Referring to the Samaritan, Jesus said, "Go and do likewise" (Luke 10:29–37). We are therefore admonished to get involved in the lives of others.

However, the lessons from Jesus and from the book of Proverbs should not leave the impression that we must attempt involvement with anyone and everyone. We are to keep our distance from some. Involvement is not indiscriminate, for the Bible states, "Do not make friends with a hot-tempered man; do not associate with one easily angered" (Proverbs 22:24). The psalmist also warns that we not fellowship with the wicked (Psalm 26:5).

We may sometimes avoid people who act or think or look and dress differently from us and defend our lack of social and spiritual involvement by appealing to the wicked neighbor argument. But that may be a misuse of the biblical admonition to avoid the wicked. In fact, most people we meet will respond favorably to kindness and cordiality if we take the time and trouble to reach out and possibly find a common interest.

In a suburban Chicago church, I was working with boys in an AWANA youth group. One evening while making home visits, I met a father who was not thrilled that I had interrupted one of his favorite cable shows. What followed were a few anxious moments, but when he realized that I was concerned about his son, he changed his attitude. Our conversation improved. A few weeks later he even began attending the church that sponsored AWANA. Despite our differences, and these were many, we were able to get along because we at first found an area of common interest, and in this case, that was his son.

Too often men don't do much to make or maintain social contact with others. Usually the entire enterprise is left to the wife. It is the wife who schedules social engagements and handles details about children and other family concerns. And if friends move away, the wife rather than the husband writes letters and emails and sends gifts to maintain the relationship.

I well remember an exception to this generalization. Several years ago, following a family move, Sue Ann and I began the sometimes pleasant and sometimes unpleasant task of searching for a church. In one church a man introduced himself to me and we had a good talk. Without being nosy, Paul Leonard, who was an U.S. Army chaplain, was genuinely interested in Sue Ann and me. A couple of Sundays later, Paul and his wife, Carol, asked us to join their family for lunch following the worship service. A few weeks later Paul asked if I would like to help him lead a large Sunday school class discussion group on the Gospel of Mark. We worked on the lessons during an early breakfast together twice a month. I'm sure our family would have joined this particular church even if Paul had not taken such a special interest in me. But I'm nevertheless glad he did.

Three years later, I was asked by the church nominating committee to serve as chairman of the church in Lincolnshire, Illinois. I shared with the committee that I would need time to consider and pray about their request. In my prayers I expressed the very sincere feeling that I was unqualified for the position. This feeling seemed to be reinforced as I studied the third chapter of 1 Timothy, the first chapter of Titus, and other related passages that made me feel even more so that I was really not qualified.

I sought the counsel of my friend Paul, who helped me see and that "my respect for the chairman's role, along with my feelings of unworthiness, were actually traits that a church leader should possess." He said I should seek the Lord's guidance rather than depend exclusively upon my own strength and reasoning. Partially due to this friend's support and confidence, I accepted the nomination and the congregation's appointment to the chairmanship. I was humbled by the responsibility and served for two years before Sue Ann and I moved to suburban Indianapolis, where I began a new job responsibility. Now all these years later I fondly well remember Paul's good counsel and confidence and friendship. He was willing to reach out with the investment of his time and attention. We all have a responsibility to involve ourselves in the lives of others.

Principle 5: Candor

Three verses from Proverbs support the principle related to candor. These are: "Faithful are the wounds of a friend" (Proverbs 27:6); "Reproof is more effective for a wise man" (17:10); and "As iron sharpens iron one man sharpens another"(27:17).

Give it to me straight. What do you really think? Is the friend who has wisdom and who will level with you or even rebuke you better than one who is insincere or speaks false words of flattery? The incisive words of a true friend may hurt your pride and feelings at the moment, but over the long haul you'll be better off having heard them. By contrast, the flattery or neglect of a false friend can bring you harm in the long run (Proverbs 29:5). Refusing to speak rebuke can also bring harm. David neglected his duty to his son Adonijah, and it ultimately and tragically cost that son his life (1 Kings 1:6).

A friend will help you face the truth even if you don't want to hear it at the moment. The candor of a friend can provide the perspective or point of view you need to make wise decisions. I believe the majority of people feel that arguments are destructive to a relationship and, therefore, differences of opinion should be kept to oneself. This is not always true. There's no such thing as a conflict-free relationship. Expressing differences does not mean that we do not respect the feelings of others. Actually, we tend to keep our feelings from those people who are only our acquaintances, rather than our close friends. This is also true of differences of opinion. We learn and grow when we listen to different ideas shared by friends.

A close friend, seeing a need, a personality flaw, or observing us making poor decisions, will not remain quiet. When Moses was struggling to create a legal social order for the nation of Israel, his father-in-law, Jethro, said, "Listen now to my voice; I will give you counsel" (Exodus 18:19). Moses was exhausted trying to settle every dispute the people could manufacture. Jethro told Moses his workload was too heavy and suggested that he teach others to be fair judges, thus speeding up the resolution of disputes.

It would have been easier for Jethro to stay out of it. Why take the risk of being ridiculed or accused of meddling or be embarrassed if Moses took offense to the advice? But Jethro cared for

Moses and for Israel and was therefore willing to be candid, and Moses listened and put into practice what his father-in-law suggested. Moses and the nation were better served because Jethro was both a caring and a courageous advice-giver.

The willingness to express your own concerns with friends is another aspect of the principle of candor. Paul the apostle, after leading a slave to the Lord, sent him back to his master, Philemon of Colossae. The slave Onesimus carried a letter from Paul in which he told Philemon to welcome this slave as he would welcome Paul himself (Philemon 17). In Matthew 16 Jesus asked the disciples what the people were saying about Him. In response, a few of His followers gave Him some safe and noncommittal answers. He then gave them a rather candid question: "But who do you say that I am?" (Matthew 16:15). Perhaps there was a long silence. Then the impulsive but devoted Peter replied, "You are the Christ, the Son of the living God" (Matthew 16:16). Peter left no doubt about his perception of Jesus. As a friend and follower, he was straight with Jesus.

Possibly the most candid statement in Scripture is Christ's response to Nicodemus in the third chapter of the Gospel of John. Cautious Nicodemus, a member of the Jewish conservative religious elite, did not want to meet Jesus during the day, so he approached Jesus during the night, while no one would be aware of his visit. He was interested in Jesus' teachings and miracles, but he did not yet understand that Jesus was the Christ, the long-awaited Messiah. With simple curiosity, Nicodemus came to speak with Jesus. The Lord cut right through to the heart of Nicodemus' problem when He said, "I say to you, unless one is born anew, he cannot see the kingdom of God" (John 3:3 RSV). Most of the conversations the Lord had with people were straightforward.

Honest, forthright speech is encouraged by biblical phrases such as "speaking the truth in love" (Ephesians 4:15); "Let your yes be yes and your no, no" (James 5:12); and "Be angry, and do not sin" (Psalm 4:4). It should be remembered, however, that candor is derived from our love and concern for another's well-being. Candor is reciprocal. We need to be willing to listen to our friends' advice to us, not just give advice to them.

Candor then, in the biblical sense, means always having the interests and well-being of the other person in mind when you speak.

Principle 6: Respect

The Bible teaches that each individual is a unique creation of Almighty God. Each of us has inherent worth and dignity, not because of what we can do but, simply and yet profoundly, because we were purposefully created by the hand of God. Therefore, we should respect the humanness of each person, realizing that God loves each and every individual.

The *American Heritage Dictionary* defines the verb *respect* as follows: "to feel or show esteem for, to honor, to show consideration for, avoid violation of, treat with deference." Aretha Franklin's version of the pop song "Respect" is about a woman demanding respect in her relationships. Many people feel that close friends no longer need to show respect or deference to each other. The Bible warns against making such a mistake.

Proverbs is rich in teachings on the importance of being respectful to close friends. Some people strain a friendship by, for example, outstaying a welcome. If I fail to show respect for my friend's need to be alone or to be with his family or simply to be away from me, I will cause harm to the relationship. There is truth to the adage "familiarity breeds contempt." We read in Proverbs 25:17, "Seldom set foot in your neighbor's house, lest he become weary of you and hate you." Powerful words, aren't they? One does not show respect when he is thoughtless or takes advantage of an intimate friendship.

A lack of respect will hinder or destroy the best of relationships. Two men I know are no longer close friends because of this issue of respect. They still speak and on occasion will spend an evening together with their wives. But the great love that existed for years between these two has vanished.

I asked each man what had happened. Tom answered, "Bill is cold and aloof. He refuses to listen to my advice. And besides, his emphasis on material things has affected his love for God." When I asked Bill about this situation; he said that "Tom had overstayed visits and was disrespecting his beliefs, violating the principle of mutual respect. He was unhappy with our middle-class lifestyle and made not so subtle comments about it. Tom would come to my house with his family, spend the weekend, eat my food, allow his kids to make a mess of our home, and finally leave with little word of thanks or help with the cleanup. The final straw came when he told my wife she was not studying the Bible correctly and should follow his method." With better communication, the rift might have been prevented or at least minimized. Close friendships take work and care if they are to be sustained.

An important ingredient in the principle of respect is the toleration of individual differences. We should try to see things from a friend's point of view. And we need to provide that friend with time and space and respect. One way to ensure a lonely life is to make little things important, be a perfectionist, and condemn others when they don't measure up. Criticism is the least effective way to have an impact upon someone. Maybe in an attempt at humor someone said, "I have the gift of criticism." It's also been said, "You're not God's sheriff." A group of ten-year-old neighborhood boys formed a club and decided they needed club rules for behavior. They wrote, "Nobody act big; nobody act small; everybody act medium." Pretty cool leadership advice, don't you think?

Part of respect is self-respect. Katherine Johnson, depicted in the movie *Hidden Figures*, was a NASA mathematician in the 1950s and was surely a pioneer for African American women. Johnson, who turned 100 years old in 2018, says simply that people are people. She says her father used to say, "You're no better than anybody else, but nobody else is better than you."

Benjamin Franklin has a well-earned reputation for being a very capable, personable eighteenth-century American diplomat, inventor, and nation maker. He's one of the most important people in the founding of our nation. When Franklin was young, he had the habit of argument, often telling friends and acquaintances about how they were wrong. Luckily a Quaker friend told Franklin that he was pushing people out of his life, that his friends found they enjoyed themselves better when he was not around. The friend told him, "You act that you know so much that no one can tell you anything." Franklin knew the candid perceptions were accurate and accepted his friend's observations. Rather than become defensive, he instead began immediately to change the way he related to others.

There is an Eastern proverb that says, "A friend is someone who warns you." The Old Testament records that "faithful are the wounds of a friend" (Proverbs 27:6 KJV). Straightforward, candid communication is always present in close, satisfying relationships. No false flattery here. When friends begin to pretend to each other, they begin to draw apart.

Christ's Example

The best illustration of friendship is given to us in the life of Jesus Christ. His interaction with others provides us with countless examples that we can hold up as our goal for dealing with other men. I hope you will read and ponder the words and deeds of Jesus recorded throughout the Gospels.

Read how Jesus called His disciples, how He related to others (even His enemies) in love, how He encouraged people to live holy and caring lives, and what He taught about the unfairness of judging others. He showed his compassion for both crowds and individuals, for adults and for children, and even for those who sinned. He revealed His humanity and vulnerability at Gethsemane. He taught us about giving to others and meeting their physical needs. He taught us how to talk with others who are different from ourselves and how to visit as a guest. He taught us how to be kind and caring. He taught us how to love as a friend.

It didn't and still doesn't matter to Jesus what your background is, for He loves unconditionally. In 1 John 4:10, the Bible tells us, "In this is love, not that we loved God, but that He first loved us and sent His Son to be the propitiation for our sins." John continues with the ultimate challenge, "Beloved, if God so loved us, we also ought to love one another" (John 4:11). Paul also, in Romans 5:6–10, comments on Christ's great love.

Our goal, then, is to love others. Indeed, what theologian Francis Schaeffer referred to as the very mark of the Christian and the command of Christ is that we love one another (John 13:34–35).1 Love is at the foundation of each of the biblical principles mentioned in this chapter. Love is at the foundation of all that is meaningful in our relationships with others.

Discussion Questions

1. What are a few ways to begin friendships? Do your responses vary depending on the personality of each potential friend or the context in which you meet?

2. List three or four major obligations you have to each of your friends. What three or four things should you be able to expect in return?

3. What rituals and or ceremonies for friendship would you be comfortable with in your personal relationships?

4. What are several dangers in saying, as Jethro did to Moses, "Listen now to me and I will give you some advice"? How can you protect against these dangers and yet practice candor?

5. How do you resolve the dilemma of both respecting the individuality of your friends and yet wanting what's best for them as you see it?

CHAPTER 7

Friendship Qualities We Look for in Others

The porcupine, whom we must handle gloved, may be respected, but is never loved.
—Arthur Guiterman

A true friend is one who overlooks your failures and tolerates your successes.
—Doug Larson

Each of us has met hundreds of individuals during our time on this earth. People enter our lives for a moment or perhaps a lifetime. Some we feel close to after even a few minutes or hours, and some we know for years but really hardly know at all.

Of all the hundreds of people you know, you probably can select just five or six individuals who have become the most important people throughout your entire life. Think of it. Just a handful from the hundreds you know who have impacted you greatly. These important people may be young or old, rich or poor, influential or unknown, and even living or dead. Why did you select these particular individuals? Despite significant differences these few may demonstrate, these precious very few people are important to you because they share common and valued fundamental characteristics that you value and hold dear. The individuals you choose possess characteristics associated with close friendships.

Why do you love and respect these individuals so deeply? Who has influenced you? Who brings joy and meaning to your life? And what is it about these few good individuals that attracts you to them, often for an entire lifetime? If someone asked you to describe why you loved someone, you wouldn't answer by describing him or her physically. What is it, then, that makes a few individuals very precious to us?

For years, while teaching different classes or conducting workshops, I have asked many people the following questions:

1. Who are the five or six most influential people in your life? These are the individuals who have had the most positive influence on your life. What is their relationship to you: friend, parent, spouse, teacher, employer, sibling, etc.?

2. Why are these individuals so important to you? What are the personality and character traits they possess that have influenced you and attracted you to them?

Two additional questions are listed for your personal interest and contemplation.

1. Do you have the same traits in yourself that you have identified and value in others?

2. What trait do you most admire in others that you do not have much of yourself?

Usually the list of valued individuals includes parents, brothers or sisters, perhaps a teacher, and close friends. The responses to the second question are often similar, centering mainly on one or more of six significant personality qualities: These are acceptance, empathy, a willingness to listen, loyalty, self-disclosure, and compromise.

These basic human traits that we value greatly when practiced can draw men together in fellowship and friendship. Each of the six requires an element of love. They therefore overlap somewhat. The following is a brief discussion of each of these six essential personal characteristics identified present within the lives of greatly valued individuals in our lives and, not surprisingly, found in abundance in enjoyable, intimate, valued friendships.

Acceptance

I was a guest on a talk show on which the popular host was someone I had for years admired and respected from a distance for the values and causes he supported and represented. I did not perform well. I was nervous and tired following a long flight and a sleepless few hours in a hotel. And despite my attempts to build a connection of respect with the host, it didn't work, and I feel I failed. He was cool and rather formal toward me. After the recording, he quickly left the studio. Even though that incident took place years ago, I still remember my feelings of rejection. We all want and need to be accepted by others whom we value, and we feel pain when acceptance is not forthcoming.

A retired man told me that he felt accepted and loved by his wife because "she doesn't hold grudges." He added, "She gets mad at me, sure, but she gets over it in a hurry." But some people never seem to forget, an essential quality in forgiving. Sure, everyone gets angry, but we need to deal with it, not let it stew for long. I heard about an annual Reconciliation Day when we can set aside our anger and hurts directed toward others and seek to make amends.

Advice columnist Ann Landers shared a story of when a woman opened an envelope she received in the mail and was startled to discover a check for $3,500 and a letter from a Pennsylvania man who had stolen her wallet containing $95 twenty years before. He had adjusted the amount for twenty years of inflation. In the letter he said, "I stole your wallet. I promised God that I would make restitution, and according to the Bible anything stolen should be returned fourfold. I am sorry for any inconvenience I caused your family." The man was ill and confined to a wheelchair. The woman considered returning the money but wisely realized that he needed to be forgiven and this restitution was his way of showing it. In her reply to the man, she wrote, "Everyone makes mistakes at some time in their lives and we all need to be forgiven."

The Bible warns, "Do not let the sun go down on your wrath" (Ephesians 4:26). The Ephesian letter also records: "Let all bitterness, wrath, anger, clamor, and evil speaking be put away from you, with all malice. And be kind to one another, tenderhearted, forgiving one another, just as God in Christ also forgave you" (Ephesians 4:31–32). To forgive, to let anger subside, is to accept others as humans capable of making mistakes. A teacher told me that anger and danger are only one letter apart. I had a driver in a car next to me raise his fist and he looked like he wanted to kill me. I was wrong in changing lanes too quickly, and I tried to express through my facial expression that I was sorry. We both went on our way, but for this stranger to exhibit such hostility reveals he likely had little inner peace.

A successful businessman once told me he wanted a divorce because his wife was no longer "interesting" to him. He had an image of what a perfect wife should be, and since his wife failed to measure up, he wanted out. His wife was a broken woman; she tried hard to measure up, but she failed, according to her husband. She needed acceptance; instead he gave her only rejection.

In numerous ways we need to get beyond the "I'm right, you're wrong" mentality. A better approach is, "We're different; let's accept that." Unity need not mean uniformity. To establish and maintain enjoyable and healthy relationships, we need to accept one another despite our differences. Carl Rogers, the noted psychologist, states that if we want to build relationships, if we want to learn to accept others, we must "destroy the idea of what a person should be." A woman constantly bugged her husband to take out the garbage until he said, "As soon as you stop nagging, I'll take it out." A woman addicted to cigarettes complained about how her husband nagged her about her habit: "I need his compassion, not his scolding." For years a father told one of his three daughters she was fat and should lose weight. She never lost a pound. What was lost was the affection between parent and child.

Few people change when they're told to change, even if it's "for their own good." When we stop trying to change people and simply accept them the way they are, even with what we might think are irritating habits, we put people more at ease. They feel loved and surprisingly, are more likely to change. They know that a part of our acceptance is wanting them to improve and to do better. It is a fact of human nature that when we know we are accepted, we are more willing to be held responsible for some things we think and do. Wisdom is sometimes learning what to overlook.

On my informal friendship surveys, people often said of an accepting friend, "He realizes he's not perfect, and I guess that makes him more willing to accept my imperfections." If we admit that we have faults, we're more likely to be sympathetic to the imperfections of others. Matthew's Gospel asks, "Why do you look at the speck in your brother's eye, but do not consider the plank in your own eye?" (Matthew 7:3).

A boy caught red-handed in mischief by his mother tearfully asked, "Do you love me anyway?" We never outgrow the need for assurance that someone truly unconditionally loves and accepts us. The key to close relationships is being loved anyway. That's acceptance.

Empathy

One comment I received on a questionnaire linked the connection of empathy to friendship: "When I have a serious problem my friend asks, 'What are 'we' going to do about it?' Can you imagine that I am so lucky as to have a friend who is willing to share problems as well as joys?" The New Testament says we should "rejoice with those who rejoice, and weep with those who weep" (Romans 12:15 RSV). We share both the ups and downs of life with those close to us.

One man told me, "Usually I don't like it when someone responds to any sad or painful situation I'm experiencing with a response, 'I know how you feel.' They don't know how I feel." This man said he was open to a close relationship. He did, however, not care for superficiality. I'm convinced that some of the deepest friendships develop during a time of sorrow. If we shrink from others when they are in need, we miss the opportunity to help, and we miss the chance to build a friendship.

A social worker was teaching an adult Sunday school class in Indianapolis. Bryon and his wife, Susan, had been close to a married couple who suddenly lost their only child in a car accident. Bryon and Susan went to the funeral home to offer help and sympathy. Instead, they simply hugged their friends and cried. Bryon and Susan may have been embarrassed with their display of emotion, but their friends will always remember the empathy expressed during their personal crisis.

Nolan and Nathan Lovas of Waukesha, Wisconsin, are identical twins. When they were just seven years old, Nolan developed leukemia. The chemotherapy treatments caused all of his hair to fall out. So that Nolan wouldn't be the only one at school with a bald head, Nathan shaved his head. The twins continued to look identical, even during the time of serious illness.

During the 1980 presidential primary season, *Newsweek* magazine told the story about George H. W. Bush. While a boy in school, the future president was with a group of boys who laughed at an obese youngster stuck in a playground tunnel. Rather than join the laughter, George ran to the boy's side and helped push him through, apparently unconcerned about what the gang might think. President Bush lived a full life of ninety-four years with service and empathy for others. A true friend will come to your aid even if it's unpopular to do so. When we are concerned with others, we tend to be less aware of ourselves. It's ironic how happiness eludes those who seek it directly. But the person who takes on the burden of concern for the welfare of another often discovers, surprisingly perhaps, that he has indirectly obtained happiness, but he's obtained happiness nevertheless.

To be empathetic is to be concerned about and to understand and to treat people as equals. A retired schoolteacher told me she can often tell if someone has a heart for children by his or her body language. The person who cares will sometimes kneel and speak to the little person at his or her level—eye to eye. Somehow people know if we truly do care about them.

While a senior in college, I substitute-taught in a third-grade class for a week at Harrison School on the west side of South Bend, Indiana. It was the custom of each student, upon entering the room in the morning, to give fifty cents to the teacher to be held for safekeeping until lunchtime. The first day I substituted for the regular teacher, one of the boys took two quarters out of the basket in the desk before we broke for lunch. At lunchtime I was short two quarters. After I quietly found out who had taken the money, I sent the other children on to lunch with another teacher. Billy had taken the money because he was hungry and had no money. He came from a broken home and was often sent to school with neither breakfast nor money for lunch. It would have been easy to chastise Billy, and it was necessary to help him see that it was wrong to take someone else's quarters.

Still, a hungry boy sat before me. The school provided a lunch for him that day and began the process of getting him into its subsidized lunch program. The next day, the children came in with their books and quarters. I had talked with Billy during a break and asked him if he would help me at lunchtime. While he was surprised, he was eager to pass out the quarters just before lunch. He was happy that someone had tried to understand him and his problems, and only Billy and I knew what had occurred the day before. Most schools no longer collect lunch money this way, but I'll always remember Billy and hope he is doing well in life.

Understanding has to do with knowing, and empathy has to do with feeling. Understanding and empathy can be and should be close allies. We need to take the time to understand and to empathize, to risk ourselves, and maybe a few quarters, to leave a positive impression upon the lives of others.

Listening

One older college student told me, "At the end of a long day of work and stuff at home, I need to talk to my husband. You know, he really listens. I love him." Another person said, "He's always willing to hear what I have to say. I never have to feel that my small problems are unimportant."

Our culture seems to suggest that talking is more important than listening. We respect and admire great orators, but who are the great listeners of our society? The question may seem odd, but nevertheless what the world needs are more listeners. Almost everyone I surveyed placed high value on a person who would be quick to listen.

We possess four basic communication skills: reading, writing, speaking, and listening. You can take a course in any one of the first three, but seldom do you ever hear of a course or learning opportunity on how to listen better. If men would learn to listen to others, many psychologists and psychiatrists might have shorter workdays.

A friend told me about a counseling session he had with a woman who was having serious problems with her husband. The problem was so distressing that my friend felt unable to offer any meaningful help. After listening to her for nearly an hour, he apologized for being unable to offer a good solution. Surprisingly, the lady responded, "You have helped me so much. I feel better now." He had helped her by simply giving to her his full attention for a few important minutes.

Sociologist Tony Campolo, author of *Who Switched the Price Tags?*, says that he gives his wife his complete attention when she speaks to him. "I hang on her every word and involve myself intensely in everything she is saying." Nothing pleases his wife more than when he listens intently and responsively.

Some people listen only for a break in the conversation so they can chime in and say what's on their mind. We can miss the point of what someone is saying because we are so concerned with what we are going to say next. We read in Proverbs 18:13 that "he who answers before listening, this is his folly and his shame."

William Gladstone and Benjamin Disraeli, British statesmen, each served as prime minister at different times during the long reign of Queen Victoria. Asked about her impressions of the two men, the queen said that when she was with Gladstone, "I feel I'm with one of the most important leaders in the world." About Disraeli she said, "He makes me feel as if I am one of the most important people in the world." She admired Gladstone, but admiration does not always lead to social closeness. The queen's comment about Disraeli was likely due to his interest in her as a person.

Good listeners have the concern and ability to ask good questions such as "How do you feel about that?" and "What do you think?" These kinds of questions show our interest in listening to a friend and opens the way for more involvement with them.

During a convention I was attending at Notre Dame University, I had the opportunity to spend several minutes alone with United States Supreme Court Chief Justice Earl Warren. The meeting is memorable all these years later, not just because he was an important public figure, but because he gave me his full attention for those brief minutes. This gentle man listened to my questions completely and then gave me thoughtful answers. I have a lasting good memory of our time together as a result. If I am asked about Chief Justice Warren, the first thought that comes to mind is that you have his undivided attention regardless of who you are.

For a number of reasons prevalent in our culture, we fail to hear the feelings and needs of our acquaintances when they speak to us. And if they perceive that we are not truly hearing, at the feeling level, they will at some point stop sharing. Even our body language can tell others if we are listening or not. Looking around the room or at your watch instead of at the person communicates a lack of interest. Sadly, some men actually try to be detached and unavailable. Our gestures and eye movements are an important part of listening.

Somehow when I'm with a physician in a medical office, I get the feeling often that the physician's time is far more important than the time of the people being seen. Maybe this is why we are called "patients." That is strange behavior for what is supposed to be a service industry. The medical industry is the only business that predictably has people habitually wait a long time before service is rendered. And I don't feel that medical personnel usually listen well. How long did you have to wait during your last medical office visit?

Recently I brought an elderly neighbor to a medical doctor's office. We were on time but had to wait a long time for service. My friend, who wasn't feeling well, waited in an uncomfortable office chair for well over an hour before finally hearing his first name called. A twenty-something woman called out in a loud voice from way across the room, "Danny." In earlier years, my neighbor owned his own machinist business and employed several dozen highly skilled craftsmen, none of whom would have thought to call him by the familiar, even childlike name "Danny." What kind of employee training and what kind of office culture produces a situation where a young receptionist or nurse calls out loudly for "Danny"?

My eighty-eight-year-old friend and neighbor should have been called sooner for his scheduled cardiology appointment. And he doesn't hear well, especially when called across a room full of people. The employee should have walked closer to where my friend was seated before speaking and my friend should have been referred to with more respect such as, "Are you Mr. Neradt?" or, "Mr. Neradt?" or, "Mr. Neradt, please." Instead, there was confusion before he entered an examination room, where the door was then closed. We then sat in the small room alone and waited for quite a while longer before a medical doctor finally entered the room and met with my neighbor for what was a brief eight minutes. I think some professions can do better, especially when providing service and timely attention for the elderly.

Years ago, following a long workday, I'd come home planning to relax. If I was not careful, and sometimes I wasn't, I'd not listen well to my wife and two children, who deserved my full attention. I needed their attention, too, and the best way to get attention is to be willing to give it.

Genuine listening is an act of recognition. It shows concern and respect. In a sense it says, "You are important to me; I care about you and what you say." That's a major ingredient in any relationship and in friendship building.

Loyalty

Many of the questionnaire responses I received pointed to the value of loyalty in a valued friend. The following were common kinds of responses I received: "When I tell Howard something in confidence, I know he will not spread it around." "He means what he says." "If my close friend thinks I'm doing something self-destructive, he'll tell me because he cares about me."

Like a precious diamond, loyalty has many sparkling facets. For instance, the loyal friend is not two-faced. Gossip is cancerous to friendships. Immature people tend to gossip to gain attention. A loyal friend avoids these destructive conversations. A loyal friend will be honest with you, and he can be trusted not to betray your confidence. A loyal friend knows that insincerity will hinder a relationship. In my home library I have a picture of dozens of beautiful old redwood trees. The caption reads, "Quality endures." Quality friendships endure the test of time mainly because of the loyalty of friends.

Commenting on his colleagues at Ford Motor Company, former CEO Lee Iacocca said that he was a hero until he was fired; then he was someone to be avoided at all costs. "I was hurting pretty bad after the firing. I could have used a phone call from somebody who said, 'Let's have coffee; I feel terrible about what happened,' but most of my friends deserted me. It was the greatest shock of my life."[1] People who responded to my questions expressed great appreciation for those who do what they say they will do, who can be counted on to follow through with promises in a timely fashion. The loyal friend honors long-range commitments, which is not easy in our fast-paced culture.

A retiree lamented that when his work ended, everything ended. He was surprised and referred to himself, somewhat despairingly, as a "FIP," that is a "formerly important person." A focus largely upon work at the expense of family and friends can be just one-dimensional and lead to aloneness, sadness, and a lack of positive and meaningful involvement in the lives of others.

Friendship can be very fragile. Two New Jersey women, who had been friends for over fifteen years, wanted to try their luck at an Atlantic City casino. When they got to the slot machines, they decided to pool their money and divide equally any possible winnings. You guessed it! On that day one of the ladies hit a jack-pot worth $327,296. But instead of sharing, the winner informed her friend that she intended to keep it all to herself. This decision led to a court battle and, of course, an end to their friendship. A trial resulted in a division of the money between the two women. When the verdict was read, the friend who brought the lawsuit said, "I would rather have had our old friendship than the money."

When Jack Whittaker from West Virginia won the $315 million Powerball, the money was supposed to be the stuff of dreams but soon turned into a nightmare. Whittaker says money doesn't bring happiness and that he no longer had any friends.

Nearly fifty years ago, in the 1970s bestseller *Future Shock*, Alvin Toffler observed that ours is a throwaway society where even friendships are temporary. Commitments to friends, job, community, country, and even family are on the decline. The resulting lack of intimacy contributes to countless personal and social problems. Juvenile delinquency, divorce, mental illness, and child abuse are only a few examples. In recent years these negative social occurrences seem to have increased.

The unfortunate irony is that many, in an effort to purge themselves of the unhappiness and loneliness caused by a lack of committed relationships including friends, actually want even more independence. We still live in the so-called me generation, a disposable society in which smart people "look out for number one." On some social media sites, including Facebook, we can "unfriend" individuals once we tire of them.

Some take assertiveness training; others demand their own rights. Some argue that this "what's in it for me" trend can presumably help people with low self-images, but overall the outcome is usually destructive if we neglect the needs of others and keep the focus mainly on ourselves.

Loyal friends are flexible and tolerant of each other's idiosyncrasies. Sometimes at stressful times, a great deal may be required from one member of a friendship. In his book *The Friendship Factor*, Alan Loy McGinnis describes a husband who had recently lost both his job and his self-confidence. He became difficult to live with and then impotent. His loyal wife, focused upon her lifelong commitment to her husband, knew he needed her now more than ever. There are periods in any relationship when one does most of the giving. It is a test of loyalty.

My wife, Sue Ann, has a friend from her high school days who was personable and intelligent. She went on to college and graduate school and eventually received a master's degree in chemistry. Soon after she began her teaching career, she married a wonderful guy. One evening, years later, she complained of a severe headache. Her husband took her to a nearby hospital, but the emergency room doctor did not feel her condition was serious. It was not until the next day, after being sent home and later going back to the hospital, that it was eventually discovered she had contracted spinal meningitis.

It's been nearly a lifetime since her husband learned that his wife would never again be her normal self. She has difficulty reasoning or doing even simple tasks. His dream of intellectual and spiritual companionship and of a normal family life never happened. Despite their circumstance, they are still together, and he loves her. He is not grudgingly meeting this responsibility, although there are bad days. Rather he is living out the commitment he made to the woman he loves. Compare this to the self-indulgent sexual playboy who dumps his partner or even spouse because she is, in his distorted view, no longer young enough or pretty enough to satisfy his adolescent macho sexual fantasies.

Most of us will not be called upon to show our loyalty to a friend or spouse by having to make great sacrifices. Regardless of our situation, we should stick by our friends. This may seem foreign to the "what's in it for me" crowd, but with the help of God and godly companionships and prayer, this is how we experience a deep residing contentment with commitment to give and receive, no matter what.

Self-Disclosure

Virtually all the respondents to the questionnaire shared that those closest to them are people who are willing to disclose their feelings and personal needs. "John called on me when he needed help. I didn't feel imposed upon; in fact, I felt privileged he turned to me. I feel I can share with him too." "Becky lets me know what her own needs are." "Marty doesn't try to pretend she doesn't have problems too." "I feel a part of his life."

We often fail to open ourselves to others out of fear of rejection. If we acted upon some of our deepest thoughts or feelings, we might end up in jail. If you open up, you take a risk, and when you share with others, you become vulnerable. Since dependency is often interpreted as weakness, men tend to fear sharing their emotions with others.

Of course, you shouldn't disclose your needs and concerns to those who are not interested or when it's obviously inappropriate. But as a relationship develops, individuals can appropriately share needs, problems, expectations, fears, wants, and even weaknesses. If you usually hide your feelings or present an unreal front, you may be viewed as unapproachable. Then friendships remain superficial.

We shouldn't be afraid to ask for help. No one wants to be a pest, but too often the "I don't want to be a burden" argument is a smokescreen we use to avoid closer relationships. An extreme and very tragic example of how far some will go before they reach out to others occurred years ago when a former Pennsylvania minister, unemployed and too proud to accept handouts, brought tragedy to his family. He rejected welfare and refused to send his children to a public school where they would have qualified for free lunch programs. His fourteen-year-old son tragically died from starvation, and his wife and other children were hospitalized for malnutrition.

Strange as it may seem at first, people feel drawn toward those who are willing to receive. We believe "It is more blessed to give than to receive" (Acts 20:35). While this injunction is surely true, it doesn't mean we shouldn't be receivers too. Many of us are stingy receivers. Jesus often began a new relationship by asking for food or lodging, or fellowship. We tend to withdraw from people who seem totally self-sufficient. With His willingness to receive, Christ gave others an opportunity to give. We like to help. We want to be useful. Talk to virtually any elderly American, and you will hear some comment about wanting to continue to be useful. We do no one a favor by removing opportunities for them to contribute to the lives of others.

A friend I valued very much was older and had accumulated a good deal of wisdom. He was kind and willing to share with me, and I was grateful for his positive influence. After a time, however, I felt somewhat uneasy. I think I now know what the problem was. I was always on the receiving end of the friendship. My friend conveyed the impression that he didn't have any needs— or at least none he cared to acknowledge with me. At best it was a lopsided relationship, like that of the Lone Ranger and Tonto. My friend wore an emotional mask that prevented me from ever doing any giving in the relationship.

When a person feels needed, he feels worthwhile. A school superintendent could not understand why the teachers in his district were grumbling and generally complaining of low morale. The superintendent wondered, "Why should they complain? After all, they are among the best paid faculty in the county." But most of the teachers did not feel needed or important or appreciated. When collective bargaining was introduced in the school system, an adversarial relationship was established. Teachers, while well paid, believed they were no longer recognized for a job well done. We never outgrow our need to be a necessary member of some group. We need to feel valued. We need to be told we're doing a good job whatever our age or position. I feel that a major reason retirement is such a difficult adjustment for most men is that they are likely to no longer have the sense of being needed.

In addition to the fear of rejection, we tend to hold people at arm's length because we want to be admired. Movie star Robert Mitchum talked long ago about his friend John Wayne. He said, "The Duke was six feet, four inches tall, but still wore four-inch shoe lifts and a ten-gallon hat." Mitchum says that Wayne once confided, "You gotta keep them Wayne-conscious." This may work for a career but not for friendship. It's difficult to be yourself and be honest in relationships when you have a desire and a noticeably focused need to be admired.

If people knew our true selves, without our social masks, they wouldn't admire us, or so the reasoning goes. It's unfortunate that in selected situations we are not more transparent. The emotionally secure individual expects to like and trust others. He also expects to be liked by others for who he genuinely is as a person. Openness produces openness. Proverbs advises that to have friends, we need to be friendly (17:17; 18:24; 27:6; 27:10). For a friendship to work, it must be reciprocal.

Compromise

Information I collected on questionnaires included comments like the following that are about compromise: "I'm glad Bob doesn't always insist on getting his own way. Bill is willing to consider what I think. Our manager is considering the ideas of others in our group and that results in better solutions."

Some men think that being firm and quick with their decisions is a sign of strength. But how can it be weakness to be sensitive and attentive to others? Many counselors believe that one sign of the mentally healthy person is when they are neither a dictator nor a doormat. We should possess and express convictions, but not to the extent that we disregard the convictions and feelings of others.

An unwillingness to compromise is often a manifestation of insecurity. A young woman said, "When I was dating, I liked being told what to do and what we were going to do. Now I'm older, and I don't like men who are rigid and insensitive to my ideas."

In Washington, D.C., there has been in recent years a daily litany of loud voices, angry disagreements, and lack of compromise both within Congress and between Congress and with the administration. The Congress and president will need to compromise if there is to be progress in the nation's business. Former Wyoming U.S. Senator Al Simpson says, "The whole attitude against compromise in Congress is crazy. If you can't compromise, don't go into business or Congress, and for heaven's sakes don't get married." The same can be said about friendships. To get anything done in this world usually requires compromise with others. Sam Rayburn, Speaker of the U.S. House of Representatives during the 1950s, once said when compromise was in short supply in Congress, that "any jackass can kick a barn down, but it takes a carpenter to build one." We have to work hard and compromise with others to accomplish most things of value.

A dictionary defines *compromise* as "a settlement of differences in which each side makes concessions." A suburban housewife in Chicago said that if her husband, just once in a while, would take her to a concert or out to dinner, she wouldn't mind spending two weeks each summer with him on a fishing trip to northwestern Wisconsin. If we compromise, others tend to compromise, allowing friendships and other relationships to develop.

Summary

We look for these six essential personal qualities of friendship in others. Now for the hard question: Do you have these traits within your own personality and within yourself? Demonstrating them in your own life will open the door for genuine friendships and indirectly a greater contribution and satisfaction with life.

Discussion Questions

1. Which qualities of friendship listed in this chapter do you and the important people in your life possess?

2. Discuss the meaning of this statement: "Friends compromise on matters of personal convenience, not on matters of personal principles."

3. In what way is listening an important communication skill in the making and keeping of friendships?

The Stages of Friendship

Be slow to fall into friendship; but when thou art in, continue
firm: and constant.
—Socrates

A friend is someone who knows all about you and still loves
you.
—Elbert Hubbard

W e are admonished to love others, but must we love all individuals with the same intensity and involvement? Should your love be somehow divided equally among the people you know? And should you feel guilty because you have failed to live up to those seemingly democratic expectations? Each of these questions deserves a definite answer of no. Scripture requires that we love others, to be sure, but this love is bound to take different forms and be expressed in many different ways and time allotments. Biblical principles of love and friendship may be applied differently, depending on how well you know and how deeply you care for and are committed to another person.

Jesus formed relationships easily with men and women as well as with children. People with different social positions and views of the world were drawn to Him. Many were aware of His love and concern for them as individuals. But despite His total love for each and every person, He nevertheless related to people differently.

Many are surprised to learn that Jesus did not treat everyone the same. From His large group of followers, Jesus felt the need to select a small group of twelve men to work and fellowship with more intimately. This important and assumingly difficult selection process was preceded by a time of prayer. Who were the men Jesus picked to work closely with Him? The apostles were a diverse group of human beings. They were not the men we have stereotyped and immortalized in stained glass. The almost effeminate and saintly mental images many harbor do not represent the men who were closest to Christ. Their real-life personalities contained flaws as well as virtues.

Most were young fishermen who labored with their hands. They had little education and surely no training in theology. Only three left a written account of their days with Jesus. The remaining nine were probably illiterate. In the entire group, there was not a priest or a single member of the upper class. These, then, were ordinary, common men who usually failed to understand Jesus' teachings and occasionally even undermined His efforts because of their own personal ambitions and lack of understanding.

Jesus developed friendships with non-perfect people, providing us with an important example. We're rather foolish and self-centered if we expect perfection from our friends. It's not about perfection within ourselves or others. It's about rather striving with the help of friends to live a consistent life, and when we fall short we ask forgiveness and simply start again. Jesus selected imperfect men, not just to advance the kingdom of God, but because, in His humanness, He too wanted fellowship. The large crowds that followed Him around Galilee could not satisfy the desire for close friendship.

Jesus developed closer relationships with the apostles than He did with other devoted followers. And within the group of

twelve there were three who shared yet even closer companionship with Him. Jesus developed a deeper stage of friendship with
Peter, James, and John than He did with the others. Even among
the three, Jesus was closer to the apostle John than to Peter or
James.

The biographical account of Christ's life provides an important example, namely that it is not only undesirable, but it's impossible to treat everyone in the same fashion. Each of us knows
many acquaintances. Each of us confides in and feels closer to
some individuals more than others. This is quite natural since
we have neither the emotional capacity nor the time to share
intimately with everyone. And not everyone we know has the
emotional energy, time, or desire to be very close to us. If we are
sensitive to this reality, it will help us overcome feelings of being
neglected by others.

Some men develop close friends rapidly. Jonathan and David
are one example. Others develop closeness over a longer period
of time, like Peter and Paul. And still others, like Job and Eliphaz,
never manage to become close friends. While the time required
to cultivate a friendship may vary, all friendships go through specific stages. And in each stage our words, thoughts, and actions
are different.

Where we are in a relationship affects how we will likely behave. Several teachers I know in Germany tell me that Americans,
myself included, are quick to meet others and find it easy to form
friendly acquaintances, but we're not very good at forming true
and lasting friendships. I found the observations interesting and
likely true that Americans are slow and find it difficult to form
genuine friendship commitments.

There are at least three distinct stages or levels of interpersonal relationships. I will refer to these different levels as acquaintance, companionship, and established friendship. This chapter
will examine each stage and suggest ways to begin and maintain
closer relationships.

Stage 1: Acquaintance

An acquaintance can be a stranger at a party or game, an interesting person we meet on an airplane, or a next-door neighbor we may have known for several years. The length of time we know an individual is not important in an acquaintance relationship. Many of us have worked for years with individuals we do not know well or feel close to particularly. These people are and probably will remain mere acquaintances.

Conversation with acquaintances is sporadic and rarely goes beyond safe and superficial topics. These could include shop talk, the best fertilizer to use on the lawn, the weather, or one's golf game. Safe topics have low emotional content and allow us to talk while, at the same time, keeping under wraps our beliefs and feelings. Subjects with high emotional content are usually inappropriate conversation topics at this level.

A relationship at the acquaintance stage is likely to be based on where we live or work rather than on common values or goals. If we move, change jobs, or shop in a different part of town, we drop our casual acquaintance relationships in the old neighborhood, at our previous jobs, or at the previous stores. Most of these relationships form because of what sociologists refer to as propinquity, or physical nearness. They quickly dissipate if we remove ourselves from day-to-day contact with the people.

In many circumstances, it is advantageous to maintain impersonal relationships. For example, business, legal, educational, and military interpersonal contacts are frequently formal and impersonal. Max Weber, the nineteenth-century German sociologist, in his classic studies of bureaucracy, recognized the wisdom of formalizing certain kinds of human interaction in order to maintain objectivity, impartiality, and equality of treatment. Theoretically, favoritism is not involved, or is at least minimized with bureaucratic decision-making. Promotions are based upon ability and merit rather than on friendship or nepotism.

But impersonality within corporate America is sometimes carried to extremes. Men who are merely acquaintances can at least exchange a brief pleasantry on occasion. One doesn't need to create a close relationship to extend courtesies to others during daily activities and routines.

A colleague of mine, Dr. Jay Thompson, emeritus professor of Ball State University, has consulted with foremen in factories to improve communication and reduce conflict between workmen at different levels of responsibility. The foremen are encouraged to apply sincere and simple psychological principles in working with the men and women on the assembly line. Such common niceties as greeting workers with a "hello" or "how's it going?" are truly appreciated. The foremen also are encouraged to praise good workmanship and to use positive rather than negative reinforcement. In short, Jay encourages these men and women to "be nice" to the people they work with. The result is a more pleasant working relationship for everyone.

There is a footnote to this story. One of the foremen told Jay, "You know, my wife and I are getting along a bit better lately." Courtesy, kindness, and thoughtfulness are principles that apply to all human relationships, regardless of the level or type of personal relationship. A Johns Hopkins School of Public Health study revealed that employees who are allowed and even encouraged to talk to fellow workers during the workday have more healthy hearts. Employees with little freedom to talk to others on the job have higher rates of heart disease. Apparently small talk with coworkers around the proverbial water cooler is good for your health.

The writer of Hebrews tells us "to show hospitality to strangers" (Hebrews 13:2 RSV). A starting point can be a smile, a greeting, a kind word, or an interested, sincere question. Phrase your questions in terms of the other person's interests. Every person has an interesting story to tell if given an opportunity to share with someone who has sincere interest.

The very least we can do at this acquaintance stage is to make a conscious effort to learn the name of our new acquaintance. Be pleasant; ask questions that reveal both interest and acceptance; listen well to what the person says. When and if you meet a second time, use his name; he'll appreciate the fact that you thought enough of him to at least remember his name. And using the name also helps you remember it. But if you don't remember his name, for sure don't try to fake it. Rather say, "I'm sorry; tell me your name again."

The key to an enjoyable, long-standing acquaintance relationship, such as with a fellow employee at work, is to be pleasant and simply treat the other person in the fashion you would expect to be treated—the Golden Rule approach. William Wordsworth wrote in his poem "Lines Composed a Few Miles Above Tintern Abbey," "That best portion of a good man's life, / his little, nameless, unremembered acts / of kindness and of love." Most acts of kindness are remembered by those who receive them. Aviator Amelia Earhart said "No kind action ever stops with itself. One kind action leads to another. A single act of kindness throws out roots in all directions."

Herb Goldberg, in his book *The Hazards of Being Male*, argues that it is extremely difficult for a man to progress beyond the first, superficial stage of interpersonal relationships. Goldberg attributes this inability to early negative conditioning: "By college days all men have already been thoroughly contaminated by the competitive posture which undermines the possibility of genuine intimacy."[1] Male relationships therefore begin and remain mainly at a manipulative surface level.

Following ten years of research, Daniel Levinson, commenting about the topic of male friendship, said that friendship was largely noticeable by its absence. Levinson concluded that close friendship with a man or a woman is rarely experienced by American men. These are strong and pessimistic conclusions expressed by both Goldberg and Levinson that remain valid conclusions in our own time. But while the relationships of most men remain at a shallow level, those who understand and apply principles of friendship can develop deeper, more meaningful relationships, if they choose to do so.

An acquaintance relationship, while lacking in emotional attachment, need not be self-serving or manipulative. On the other hand, relationships do remain shallow if the parties are interested only in them for self-serving reasons. Men may progress to higher levels of relationship if they know and apply biblical principles of friendship. Proverbs 18:24 says that "a few close friends are more valuable than a host of acquaintances." This is true, but it's also true that all close friendships were at one time mere acquaintances. We shouldn't underestimate our opportunity to find companions or friends from people who are now only acquaintances. Someone once said that we speak of neutral things and take a long time to be at ease with each other, and let years go by just as if we had five lifetimes in which to be friends and could afford to squander this one. Sometimes acquaintances become something more.

Stage 2: Companionship

If acquaintances hit it off and are able to communicate and share something in common, they form what may be termed a companionship. Sharing something in common is a vital ingredient to a companionship. At this stage, men share common goals rather than common core values. Together men join teams, flirt with girls, and go off to school or some engage in work or some other activity. Their togetherness is often based on a task to be performed or a goal to be obtained. Men can come comfortably close to each other when they are sharing a common target or goal or task.

Researchers Edward Shils and Morris Janowitz, in 1948, conducted a study of the cohesion and disintegration of the German army. Although outnumbered and being beaten badly, the

German soldiers late in World War II fought on with great effec-
tiveness. Many attributed their tenacity to their strong political
convictions. The study revealed, however, that the commitment
to continue fighting was related to membership in a small squad.
As long as the squad members both gave and received affection
within the group, they were prepared to fight regardless of their
individual political attitudes. Being buddies or companions sustained them because of common goals or a feeling of belonging
rather than common values.

Americans are certainly group-oriented. We're big on joining
groups. Men have always embraced many voluntary associations,
including the ancient gathering of freemasonry. Recent examples
of popular voluntary male associations are fraternal and service
organizations, country clubs, weekly poker parties, sports bar
meet-ups, and even youth gangs.

Unlike acquaintances, companions schedule time together.
They go beyond the "Hi, how are you?" syndrome that's associated with happenstance meetings. Buddies enjoy each other's
company, and although the relationship may exist for many
years, usually it is based largely on the immediate and limited
satisfactions that come with companionship. Two men I know
have played golf together on a regular basis for years. They enjoy the togetherness of playing a game, but they make few comments that are not related to the game of golf or something such
as professional baseball or football. They truly do not know each
other well but are able nevertheless and ready to enjoy the satisfaction that comes from companionship. Unlike women, men
are more able or perhaps I should say more willing to relate to
selected segments or aspects of another person's life. Women in
contrast usually assume a holistic approach to the complete human personality.

This companionship level of relationship, while satisfying and
even intense at times, will not stand up well to emotional stress
or individual conflicts regarding values or interests. There is

little commitment in a companionship, as each man knows that if a real problem occurs, he cannot or will not turn to the companion for assistance. Men do not seek out a buddy when they need help in time of a personal crisis. This is especially true for men of marginal economic status, as William Whyte and Elliot Liebow have researched and eloquently written about in the classic studies *Street Corner Society* and *Talley's Corner*, both of which I read when I was in college. Steve Sabol, who conducts the Knights of the 21st Century ministry, states, "Companions don't cost much and can be easily found. We can't rely on them for help, support, or even encouragement in time of need."

Last fall one of the attorneys in our community was quite ill and required emergency surgery. For several days, he was in rather serious condition. When he was finally able to again play golf, his golfing companion said to the nearly recovered man, "I hear you were quite ill. Is everything okay now?" The fortunate man responded, "I'm just fine. In fact, I'm so good, I'll beat you today."

They both laughed and that was it. Nothing else was said about the illness. It's strange somehow that the man, when sick, had made no effort to communicate with his companion. And the companion, when hearing of the illness through the clubhouse grapevine, made no effort to contact his buddy. Then, with the interruption behind them, both were willing to reassume their regular weekly or biweekly round of golf.

Despite the lack of a long-range commitment, companionships serve the important function of providing fellowship. They give the warm feeling of belonging, similar to The Three Musketeers credo: All for one and one for all.

Lovie Smith, head football coach at the University of Illinois, was asked why he returned to coaching NFL football in 2014 to his former team, the Tampa Bay Buccaneers, where he had worked previously with Tony Dungy. In 2013, Smith had been fired by the Chicago Bears after nine seasons. He talked about his love of the team and of Tampa Bay. He also said that "the emotional aspects of the game are stronger and positively more challenging than anywhere else I know." Many NFL players enjoy and value the relationships when on a team and may have some difficulty adjusting to their post-playing years without the companions on the team. Companions give a man a feeling of confidence about his value as a man.

Companionship may not be friendship, but it is a type of relationship we need. You can deepen a relationship by making an effort to learn more about the men you know as companions. It isn't inappropriate, if the situation is right, to ask probing, sincere questions that are thoughtful and other-person centered. If a buddy wants to share a problem, we should listen well.

Companionships need nourishment, for they, like other levels of interpersonal relationships, can be fragile. There are, for example, two problems that can get in the way of beginning and maintaining a companionship. These problems are trust and dominance. We can recognize the kinds of behavior that could destroy the confidence we have in each other. And each of us can consciously work toward equalizing power and decision-making so that neither ends up in the shadow of the other.

Men have frail egos and rarely work at improving a relationship. We turn off with the slightest provocation and conceal our true selves from others. Few acquaintances or companionships therefore evolve into actual friendships. While true friendships may be a rarity, they can be developed if we are willing to invest the necessary time and emotional energy.

Stage 3: Established Friendship
Some men seek more than just a buddy relationship. Companions who share basic similar values and who invest the necessary time and attention may go on to establish friendships.

In Chapter 6, we surveyed biblical principles of friendship, including the following six principles: 1) worldview centered upon God, 2) formation of a covenant, 3) faithfulness, 4) social involvement, 5) candor, and 6) respect. And we reviewed friendship examples the Lord provides. In Chapter 7, we surveyed six friendship qualities, including 1) acceptance, 2) empathy, 3) a willingness to listen, 4) loyalty, 5) self-disclosure, and 6) compromise. These biblical friendship principles and friendship qualities are closely related and provide the essential ingredients for established friendships.

In this section, we will consider the forming and primarily the maintenance of established friendships. The way we acquire a friend is very similar to how we keep a friend. How do we best pay attention to making and keeping friendships? "I know that the dissolution of a personal friendship is among the most painful occurrences in human life." So wrote Thomas Jefferson to James Monroe. The ancient Roman Seneca said, "To lose a friend is the greatest of evils." What factors lead to a cooling off or ending of a friendship? A friendship can change or even end when one moves, gets married, has a child, gets divorced, becomes much richer, becomes much more successful, changes political views, borrows money, or decides to take a vacation together.

These responses, while interesting, do not reveal the symptoms of a dying friendship, but rather seem to indicate a sudden breaking off of the relationship. C. S. Lewis noted that people do not suddenly renounce their faith in God due to some event or newly acquired insight. Rather, over a long period of neglect, the once-strong relationship between man and God slowly dies. I believe this same process of neglect describes how a friendship between friends dies.

Alex and I and our wives were good friends. Alex was my friend of many years who believed we should be of one mind on any issue of consequence. We would discuss and argue, usually without resolution. I remember sharing with him from my heart the following comments: "I'm concerned that almost every conversation we have had in recent months results in either a serious political and or biblical argument. I think we can work at this and learn to get along better. I commit to trying to listen better and trying to keep my mouth shut sometimes when I disagree with you. I do know we are different and have different beliefs and have different ways of engaging the world. I think that is okay."

Alex didn't think disagreement was okay and would say we should biblically be of "one mind." It was nevertheless a surprise when he told me that he was ending our relationship. In some ways I felt relief; a friendship should not be so full of problems, difficulties, and misunderstandings. While a few years have now gone by, I still am sad and feel a sense of loss. I feel I somehow failed.

Close friends must consciously establish and renew their commitment. Commitments are not popular today. They imply inconvenience. We are bombarded with a self-indulgent, hedonistic ethic that centers on self rather than others. This aspect of our culture works to undermine our friendships. Commitment is not popular, and it may be a burden, but it is essential to the care and feeding of a friendship.

At a shopping center, I saw a girl wearing a T-shirt that read "If it feels good, do it." It's difficult for me to understand how a woman of any age could display such a phrase without embarrassment, even if she was unaware of its sexually suggestive connotation. This phrase illustrates the value system of our age, and it is rather mild when compared with some that are more vulgar. The message on the T-shirt implies that "I'll do whatever pleases me, and if my pleasure gets in your way—too bad for you." This self-centered value system is the antithesis of the commitment needed to sustain friendship.

Commitments develop slowly and logically. Commitment is not irrational. It would be foolish to trust a foothold you had not properly tested or to marry a person you have not adequately assessed or to trust an important message from a stranger you have not investigated. But commitment requires more than reason. It requires an act of faith. With the investment of faith, the sense of risk fades and hope grows.

Misfortune often provides an opportunity for a test of commitment. When friends come to our aid or defense in time of need, the relationship between us grows more secure and satisfying. We tend to reveal our true colors during times of stress. This truth is illustrated in one of Aesop's Fables, *Two Travelers and a Bear:*

Two men were traveling in company through a forest, when, all at once, a huge bear crashed out of the brush near them. One of the men, thinking of his own safety, climbed a tree. The other, unable to fight the savage beast alone, threw himself on the ground and lay still, as if he were dead. He had heard that a bear will not touch a dead body. It must have been true for the bear sniffed at the man's head awhile, and then, seeming to be satisfied that he was dead, walked away. The man in the tree climbed down. "It looked as if that bear whispered something in your ear," he said. "What did he tell you?" He answered, "That it was not at all wise to keep company with a fellow who would desert his friend in a moment of danger."

Women retain more friends than men, because while males share activities, women who are friends exchange confidences. Why? Perhaps because men may be more aware of the risk of being judged when they confide in friends. I remember painfully a friend who shared with me in confidence a serious problem. I was involved in his life and concerned about his well-being. Knowing this, he took a risk and became vulnerable. However, I reacted too strongly to the problem he confided to me and I nearly lost a friend.

The problem was infidelity. When he approached me, he no longer was participating in the adulterous relationship. He was then trying to work through his feelings of guilt. He had asked God to forgive his sin, but somehow the memory, including the mental pictures. just wouldn't go away. It was stuck in his head. He opened up to me, wanting counsel and acceptance. Unfortunately, I did not follow the Bible's directive for this type of situation: "Brethren, if a man is overtaken in any trespass, you who are spiritual restore such a one in a spirit of gentleness" (Galatians 6:1). Gentle? Not me. Supercilious is a more accurate description of my behavior.

I hardly heard a word he said. It never entered my mind that it must have been difficult for him to tell me about his sin and guilt. I was too busy moralizing to see his guilt and his pain. I exerted little effort trying to understand how he got himself into this moral predicament. Listening and showing honest Christian love would not have minimized the seriousness of the sin, but it might have helped a friend as he wanted so badly to seek forgiveness and hopefully with counseling eventually reestablish his marriage. Friends must resist being judgmental. In this situation, my friend's wife forgave her husband but they didn't quite resume their lives on the same terms. Someone said, "Even if they patch it up together, the patches will show."

Close friends have love for each other. In one study, a full 92 percent believed that friendship is a form of love. The greatest comment on love in all the Bible is recorded in 1 Corinthians 13:4–8. As you read this wonderful section of Scripture, you might consider how this section could apply to a friendship. Here it is from *The New English Bible*:

> Love is patient; love is kind and envies no one. Love is never boastful, nor conceited, nor rude; never selfish, nor quick to take offence. Love keeps no score of wrongs; does not gloat over other men's sins but delights in the truth. There is nothing love cannot face; there is no limit to its faith, its hope, and its endurance. Love will never come to an end.

Acclaimed historian Stephen Ambrose would agree that friendship is a form of love when he wrote the following in a good book that celebrates friendships among men:

> Friendship is different from all other relationships. Unlike acquaintanceship, it is based on love. Unlike lovers and married couples, it is free of jealousy. Unlike children and parents, it knows neither criticism nor resentment. Friendship has no status in law.... But freely entered into, freely given freely exercised.... Friends glory in each other's success and are downcast by the failures. Friends minister to each other, nurse each other. Friends give to each other, worry about each other, stand always ready to help.[2]

Close friends provide support during trials as well as during accomplishments. Friends even help each other to accomplish life goals. Friends respect each other's individuality and independence. While remaining available, friends do not become careless with the other's need to be alone, either physically, emotionally, or spiritually. A close friend knows the real you and loves you anyway.

In earlier chapters, I mentioned that people, regardless of gender, need emotionally supportive relationships. We all have emotional needs, which if unmet, leave us unhappy or, in the extreme, even physically or mentally ill. And yet many of us resist these relationships even though they are in our own best interest. This may be one of our biggest difficulties, the unwillingness to let other people love us. We would rather "tough it out" or "hold our own" or "take it like a man." Many men, even those who apply biblical principles, tend to go it alone when they have problems.

There is a difference between taking responsibility for our lives and trying to live independently from both God and others. I know full well that I'm responsible for going to work, paying our bills, and caring for my family. Patrick Morley states that a focus upon independence can really be rebellion against the influence of God. The independent man thinks, "I want to do what I want to do, when I want to do it, whenever I want to do it, with whomever I want to do it. I want to be in control. I want to satisfy my ambitions. I don't want to be dependent on anyone. People let me down. God will let me down. I can make it on my own. If I can be independent, then I will not need to rely upon anyone else. I will not have to trust anyone else, and I will be able to avoid the pain of being disappointed and disillusioned. If I can be independent, then I can be in control of my own life. I will have the power, whether through money or influence, to get my own way; I will have the freedom to come and go as I please."[3]

A man may not be in open rebellion from God but simply doesn't seek or want His counsel and shuns His advice. This is the "I want to do my own thing" lifestyle. The man who does not trust God trusts rather in himself and the ever-changing philosophies that may be popular at the moment.

I had lunch with my neighbor who told me he was concerned about the go-it-alone lifestyle and agnostic worldview of each of his three sons. He wondered what to share with each of them to show them that God was real, that He existed and had a rightful claim on their lives. I listened, and I then said that maybe the real issue had less to do with a need to demonstrate convincing evidence for God. Perhaps the reason these sons were apart from God was not because of a lack of reasonable evidence, but rather because each wanted to be captain of his own fate, in full control of his own life. In a sense each wanted to be his own god, and no amount of apologetic evidence and prompting from their father was likely going to change that. We can be available to listen, and we can pray and ask that the Spirit of God reaches their hearts and wills and brings each of them to Himself.

We may have a latent fear of being accused of being too close to another man. More likely we as men have simply been raised to believe that masculinity and independence are synonymous. We are often too proud to seek help or accept demonstrations of love. We know that if we accept love, later we may feel obligated to return love at a time when it may be or at least seem to be inconvenient. So instead of receiving or giving, we withdraw and withhold and, in the process, lose out.

At a men's ministry conference where I was speaking, a man gave me the following story with the source unknown:

> Within each man is a dark castle with a fierce dragon to guard the gate. Living in this castle is a lonely self, a self most men have suppressed, a self they are afraid to show. He's protected by an armored knight who keeps outsiders at sword's length even those who manage to slip by the dragon and sneak into the castle.
>
> When men take a risk, cage the dragon, give the knight some time off, lower the drawbridge, and let down the barriers, they begin to respond to others as whole persons and try to communicate with openness and intimacy. Their openness brings opportunity for a growing relationship, for a wider range of deeply felt experiences. This is the stuff from which friendships are formulated and sustained. The results are joyful, satisfying, and very meaningful.

Discussion Questions

1. Personal needs and flaws are revealed when two men become friends. Discuss whether you accept the limitations of others or expect something approaching perfection. Remember, Jesus established friendships with imperfect people.

2. Christ had friendships with people of different backgrounds and personalities. Is this true for you? Should it be?

3. How do you explain the seemingly contradictory feelings of fear of closeness and the desire for closeness? Do intimacy and commitment put you off somehow? Why or why not?

4. How should you respond when a friend confides in you that he has done something wrong, that he has sinned? Consider Galatians 6:1 as you formulate your response.

CHAPTER 9

Friendship in Other Times and Places

Do unto others as you would have them do to you.
—Luke 6:31

*A friend is one to whom one may pour out all the contents
of one's heart, chaff and grain together, knowing that the
gentlest of hands will take and sift it, keep what is worth
keeping, and with a breath of kindness, blow the rest away.*
—Arabian proverb

Is friendship the same wherever you go? Do people understand friendship to mean something specific, or does the
word have very different meanings depending on one's culture or perhaps one's period in history? We know that the family as a social institution exists in all societies. Revolutionary
societies have consistently failed when they tried to alter significantly or eliminate family structure. The family is one of God's
creation ordinances that existed before the fall of humankind
and exists today in every culture and in every nation. But what
about friendship?

Friendship is ubiquitous in history and culture. It is integral to
the psychological, social, and spiritual health of individuals and
societies, as is the family. Friendship, like marriage and family,
is a gift to us from the Lord. It is for us to protect, nurture, and

enjoy. We often let nationalistic, social, and cultural differences and prejudices cloud the reality that we are but one human race created by a loving God. In Acts 17:26 we read that "from one man he made every nation of men." Our basic emotions and our basic needs are universal.

Anthropologists have studied several tribes that seem much different from our Western culture. People in every observed tribe and nation showed a need to reach out to others, a need to make social contact and to form friendships. The similarity of humanity is equally evident from a sample reading of authors throughout history, including Aristotle, Plato, Cicero, Homer, Montaigne, Pascal, Goethe, Shakespeare, Schiller, and C.S. Lewis. Letters and diaries of average people written generations ago reveal the same feelings and spiritual and other needs we experience today.

Friendship Across the World

Several early cultural anthropologists, including Cora Du Bois, consistently agreed about many things related to friendship from their extensive cross-cultural research. I found the following points about friendship from different cultures in my personal anthropology class and research notes.

- Friendship is a universal phenomenon. Not every person has the social opportunity to develop a friendship, but friendship as a relationship occurs in all societies.
- Friendship is affected by many factors, including marriage, sexuality, kinship system, and superordinate-subordinate relationships.
- Friendships are voluntary in that they are not imposed by the culture or ascribed at birth.
- Friendships are reciprocal. The action of giving and taking flows both ways.

- Friendships are dyadic. The most widely valued type of friendship is between two people.
- Friendships are characterized by confidence, trust, and intimacy. The bonding relationship of friendship is an important characteristic of all human cultures.
- Friendships exist between two people. History records effort after effort to establish communes or utopias on the basis of intimate fellowship.

While the behaviors and norms associated with friendship may vary as one travels from culture to culture, there is throughout the world an underlying similarity of beliefs and values about friendship. In most cultures, friendship includes closeness, solidarity, absence of ulterior ends, reciprocity, and a playing down of social distinctions such as age, sex, and social status. Friendship obligations and rights are secondary to others such as family responsibilities. And yet friendship is intimate, important, and enduring. Friendship may be associated by rites of passage or ceremony and involve the exchanging of gifts or economic support.

In most cultures, friendship involves voluntary commitment, intimacy, and spontaneity, and it is valued by the society as a source for personal growth and security. Despite differences in customs, every known culture places an important emphasis upon the love and loyalty between friends. It appears that affection and loyalty are implicit in all friendships in all societies. Undivided loyalty and altruistic love are valued highly throughout the world.

Cultural Universals

In an historical reference book, *The Proper Study of Mankind*, author Stuart Chase in the 1950s cataloged thirty-three cultural universals of all humankind that have been consistently present over time. A cultural universal is an aspect of human behavior that is demonstrated in virtually every culture on the planet. Think of it. Despite the tremendous apparent outward diversity of behavior among the hundreds, perhaps thousands, of different cultures within the world's approximately 195 nations in 2019, we share much in common. Following is a sample of these universal culture traits:

1. A form of religion and ethics prevails.
2. There is an established government and laws.
3. There is a permanent family structure; monogamy is the usual form of marriage.
4. The family cares for the aged as well as the young.
5. Divorce is recognized but not approved.
6. Society provides punishment for infringement of its rules.
7. The male is usually the formal leader of the family and of society.
8. Free giving is a high virtue.
9. There is a sense of loyalty to the nation or tribe or extended family.
10. None of the societies has complete communal ownership of property.
11. Friends are usually among individuals of the same sex.1

Friendship is one of the universal cultural traits. In most cultures, a man feels a sense of shame if he lacks an intimate friendship. Aristotle reflected this feeling when he said that "without friends no one would choose to live." A little extreme perhaps, but there is a universal belief in the importance of friendship. You may be surprised by the final statement, the last universal mentioned above. Probably no greater restriction exists upon friendship than that it must be limited to individuals of the same sex. Both cross-cultural and historical information show that in nearly every culture on earth, both present and past, cross-sex friendships have not been cultivated. They may exist, but they are not overly common. But have things changed today? Can't men and women be close intimate friends?

The common belief is that men and women can be lovers but rarely friends. There is evidence that many men attempt to develop cross-sex friendships with the hope that such a friendship would lead to sex. Sociologist Robert Bell found that in cross-sex friendships, the men were usually older and better educated and they usually wanted the relationship to end up in the bedroom. A high degree of sexuality was either implied or expressed in cross-sex friendships. Furthermore, these cross-gender relationships were usually superficial and ritualistic. Could this still be true in today's world?

The #MeToo movement intends to expose the rampant sexual harassment by powerful men, first in Hollywood, journalism, and politics and now in every industry. Wheaton College in Illinois hosted a #Church-Too movement as an offshoot of the #MeToo movement. Speakers included Beth Moore, Max Lucado, Eugene Cho, Christine Caine, and Nancy Beach, who worked closely with megachurch founder Bill Hybels at Willow Creek Community Church near Chicago. Hybels was accused by several women, including Beach, of inappropriate behavior and retired in 2018. Beach asks, "Can men and women work together without falling into sexual sin?" Aimee Byrd says others are to be valued and respected rather than simply considered as temptations to be avoided.[2] In 2019 a joint newspaper investigation by the *San Antonio Express-News* and *Houston Chronicle* conducted a six-month investigation and published accusations about dozens of church leaders accused of sexual misconduct.

There have been several articles published about unintended consequences of #MeToo that may hurt both sexes. Some men are so concerned about possible repercussions from what they might say or do that they are keeping their distance from women in the workplace. With the people I interviewed, I found that approximately three-fourths of the respondents believed that cross-sex platonic friendships were complicated due to sexual tensions, the lack of encouragement by society, and the fact that men and women have less in common with each other than they do with friends of the same sex.

If either member of a cross-gender friendship is married, many respondents felt that something must be wrong or missing from that marriage. Why else would someone of the opposite sex other than the spouse be needed for close emotional involvement? A spouse is bound to feel concerned or even threatened by a close cross-sex friendship, partially due to the emotional intimacy and the potential for physical intimacy.

It is true in a few cultures, including our own, where women are highly valued and highly skilled and daily accessibility to members of the opposite sex exists in virtually every area of life. Ours is a culture where cross-gender platonic friendship is culturally encouraged. Therefore cross-sex friendships can and do exist, remain nonsexual, and provide emotional satisfaction. From my own survey and informal research, however, such emotionally satisfying cross-gender friendships in the United States remain rare.

Where cross-sex friendships exist at all, they tend to be limited to young, unmarried people. Again, from my questionnaires and conversations with men and women, I found few who believed close friendships between men and women existed that had no courtship or sexual implications.

In our society, our social lives are based on pair relationships, either as marriage partners or as same-sex friends. We have same-sex work and civic and neighborhood and church relationships. In some less-frequent cases, we might experience cross-sex platonic companions, or "buddies." But I suspect that even now, with something approaching gender equity in American society, there remain few true platonic and yet emotionally intimate friendships among individuals of the opposite sex.

It seems, from a review of different and especially simpler cultures existing in earlier centuries, that men and women came together either when it was time to work in the fields or time to eat or time to sleep. Throughout American history, the major taboos against cross-sex friendship have been based on the belief that predatory older or more socially prominent men were likely to be seeking simply a sexual conquest. This continues today, especially as we've seen recently in the entertainment industry and also in state and national governments. Many women have come forward saying they have been groped or even raped by men, usually older, in positions of power and influence, most notably in government and the entertainment and news and journalism and government industries.

Literally dozens of well-known men in these and other industries were outed by women who told of being sexually abused, assaulted, or even raped. It's no longer shocking, even when a porn star goes on a program such as *60 Minutes* and accuses the president of our country of engagement in sexual flings and claims to have even been threatened physically to discourage public disclosure of an affair before our national election. Donald Trump has denigrated women throughout his career. The eight out of ten evangelicals who voted for Donald Trump formed an unlikely, odd, and I feel, Faustian alliance with him. I remember evangelical Jim Wallis, CEO of *Sojourners* magazine, suggesting that "It is always ordinary people who come together in a social movement with spiritual values that change society more than politicians do." Messiah College teacher John Fea believes Christians supporting Trump should replace fear and power politics and unrealistic nostalgia with hope and humility and a factual history.[3]

My friend Charley Dunn referred to the recent and abundant revelations of the abuse of women often by men in positions of influence as a "sexual harassment tsunami." Oprah Winfrey would concur, saying that sexual harassment was widespread in our culture where the abuse of women ranged from the creepy to the criminal and that hopefully we are at a watershed moment when women will no longer have to put up with sexual attacks. Unfortunately, it's not always easy to discern culpability. In 2018, before the U.S. Senate Judiciary Committee. the whole nation experienced Dr. Christine Ford's accusation that nominee to the Supreme Court Justice Brett Kavanaugh sexually attacked her at a party when they were both in high school. Both Kavanaugh and Ford made compelling presentations, but at the end of the day everyone was left not knowing what had occurred years before in a hearsay, "he says, she says" standoff.

Jesus did not in any way minimize or discriminate against women. On the contrary, during a time when women suffered discrimination, Jesus treated women with respect and dignity. Godly women were influential in Jesus' life and ministry. These included Elizabeth, Mary, Anna, the sinner of Luke 7:36–40, Mary Magdalene, Martha, and Mary of Bethany, and the women at the empty tomb. While Jesus related very well to women, He nevertheless formulated His most intimate friendships with men: Peter, James, and John in particular.

Two Arminian Christian female teachers came to me one Sunday morning in a private school in Riyadh, Saudi Arabia, where we were all working. They smiled and whispered, "Christ is risen." I responded to these women, "Christ is risen indeed." Sunday is a workday in much of the Middle East, but this was Easter Sunday. No surprise there were no church bells since there were and still today are no churches allowed. These two teachers, along with several other Christians and I, had dinner that Sunday and talked about Christ and His glorious resurrection. There were both men and women in this group of Christians and the gender of those present didn't matter. Our contacts with either men or women usually require the same courtesies and respect and expectations.

Privacy or Community

Some conclude that we may be the loneliest people on earth. The book *Bowling Alone*[4] is partially a discussion of how Americans distrust government and to some extent each other. In the fifteen years since this book was originally published, our distrust of our fellow citizens and neighbors has intensified. The American themes of independence and privacy and distrust were evident even in the 1920s and 1930s and were well summarized in the seminal research of the *Middletown* and *Middletown in Transition* studies. Incidentally, in our time, Facebook and Equifax and other recent social media and credit controversies have eroded the sense of protection of our personal information. This may contribute to our feeling more vulnerable and exposed to malware and scammers.

In most societies, people do not experience loneliness, at least to the nagging, acute degree that some Americans do. In other cultures, people are rarely alone either physically or emotionally. Relatives, neighbors, and even strangers are a normal part of everyone's life. After I retired, I had the opportunity to work in many Middle East countries, including Saudi Arabia, United Arab Emirates, Lebanon, Egypt, and Syria, where I experienced in each of these and other countries the most generous hospitality with work and social and family gatherings. I remember one weekend in Syria before the tragic civil war when I had nothing planned. One of my hosts took me to my hotel after work to get a bag and then to his home, where I spent the weekend. With his wife and children, I joined them for all activities. They took several hours to give me a thorough tour of their city of Aleppo. This took place before the civil war in Syria. I'm surprised at my quick willingness to accept their hospitality, but I did—because they were so genuine and open and friendly.

In the United States, we seem to have more of an emphasis on privacy than is evident in other cultures. I know a school principal who divorced his wife two years ago after their children were grown. Now he has few responsibilities at the end of the workday. He lives in an urban community some distance from his school district, and he has no commitment to his community. "I have nothing to live up to," he told me, "and no one to please or do anything for or with after 4:30 p.m. in the afternoon every single day. I can do as I please with my time, my money, and my relationships." He told me these things seemingly with neither concern nor regret.

In most cultures, the image of a private, independent life denotes sadness. But in America, we may envy the freedom that comes with a less hectic private lifestyle. Bachelors, like the school principal who lives alone, are frequently seen as carefree, when in reality they are often lonely.

My daughter was in a weather-related accident in Michigan. I learned from her trucking company what hospital she was in and I tried to reach her, but she was sedated and could not talk on her cell phone at that time. I then asked the floor nurse in charge if my daughter was stable and would be okay. The nurse told me nothing about my daughter and said only that the federal HIPAA Privacy Law (Health Insurance Portability and Accountability Act) and the U.S. Office of Civil Rights prevented her from telling me absolutely anything about the person I was asking about. I therefore spent unnecessarily a few anxious hours not knowing how injured she was. This application of the HIPAA law is an example of privacy rights gone to seed when a concerned parent cannot even be reassured with a simple, "She'll be okay and will be able to talk with you in a few hours."

Loneliness can be included in the long list of nagging contemporary societal problems. Loneliness and a lack of commitment to others are likely correlated along with our high suicide, divorce, alcoholism, opioid drugs, murder, rape, and abortion rates. Loneliness is painful. Even the most reserved people, because of loneliness, may look for companionship through online sources and dating sites that market the promise of bringing people together.

People from other cultural backgrounds may find it difficult to understand why we so cherish personal freedom. To them, personal independence, to the extent we seek it, is viewed as a form of isolation or of being ostracized. With the songwriter of the Janis Joplin rock tune "Me and Bobby McGee," some might agree with the lyric that "freedom is just another word for nothing left to lose." Theologian Francis Schaeffer used to say that the pursuit of Americans was mainly centered upon personal peace and privacy. Today Schaeffer might add prosperity to his short list of American preoccupations.

Many Western nations, including the United States, have to some degree sacrificed emotional intimacy on the false altar of personal freedom. Many American males have never experienced a close male friendship or known what it means to care for or confide in a male friend. Those who do have friends usually have experienced low levels of trust and personal sharing and generally invest little in these relationships.

The parable of the rich fool (Luke 12:16–20) that I mentioned in an earlier chapter has several applications for us. The man, for example, was a fool because of his inordinate emphasis on materialism. This emphasis makes it difficult to provide the time and attention to the cultivation of friendships. His belongings represented his self-worth and importance. It was all about him and his stuff and his sense of self-importance.

The rich fool would feel more at home in mainstream America than in many other cultures that are less materialistic and perhaps more caring. For example, he would feel out of place if he were living with the historic Zuni Indians of New Mexico where cooperation was more the social norm and even economic norm. Emphasis is devoted to developing relationships, not to competition and the accumulation of wealth. With the Zuni, and in a handful of other cultures, the respected people were and are cooperative, friendly, and generous with time and possessions. They are not concerned with accumulating more goods or property than they and their family can use, and if they do acquire wealth beyond what is needed for their family, they are expected to share some of the gain with others.

Intimacy and Culture

The making of close friends has not received much in the way of social encouragement. Our cultural focus is mainly with the marriage and family structure. In America we are not even sure how to define friendship. To many men, the term *friend* lacks nuance and content. It is devoid of emotion and commitment. We rarely know what someone means when he declares, "He is my friend." After all, many of us have used the word to refer to someone who seems to be a pleasant fellow since first meeting him a short time ago.

Jesus, in chapter 3 of Mark's Gospel, seems to extend and even redefine our kinship responsibilities and relationships to include friendship. During a conversation, a group of people told Him that his mother and siblings were outside waiting for Him. His response was, "Who is My mother, or My brothers?" Looking around the room He added, "Here are my mother and my brothers! For whoever does the will of God is my brother and my sister and mother" (Mark 3:31–35).

It is a stretch to conclude that marriage alone can satisfy all of an individual's emotional needs. Without friends, a wife and husband must rely totally upon each other for emotional and spiritual support. Some Christian marriages collapse under the weight of this difficult demand. It's not practical or even possible to expect our wives to meet all of our emotional needs. It's not fair either.

The church could equip Christians with more than just the "how-to's" of marriage. The church mission might also encourage other long-term, supportive relationships such as friendships. For example, a church might start an "adopt a grandparent" program, where friendships can grow between generations and where everyone benefits. We can help connect younger people with possible mentors. We can grow our own extended families where we all benefit, especially our children.

There will always be a need for caring and trusting friendships. We all need a precious few individuals with whom we can be open and reveal our most sincere feelings. There is something amiss in a culture that neglects friendship, including the human bonds that are so important to our physical, psychological, and spiritual health and happiness.

Of course, we don't have to emulate friendship customs from cultures that differ significantly from our own, any more than we should begin to wash dirt from people's feet as Jesus did for the disciples. Our culture and customs are different. Our time in history may be different. Rather than copy friendship practices of other cultures, we can possibly learn from them, and then within our own culture search for ways to practice biblical principles of friendship daily. In the next chapter, we will look for additional practical ways to apply biblical principles of friendship.

Discussion Questions

1. How can cross-cultural information help us better understand the human nature God has given to us, including our need for friendship?

2. Why did Jesus select only men as His closest friends and disciples?

3. Are male/female relationships different in the twenty-first century? How does the move toward equality in the workplace and community affect relationships between men and women?

4. Do you have a desire for personal privacy and independence that is stronger than your desire for community and involvement in the lives of others?

5. Should friendship in the United States receive more social recognition, similar to marriage and parenting roles and responsibilities?

CHAPTER 10

Understanding Yourself

*Walk with the wise and become wise, for a companion of
fools suffers harm.*
—Proverbs 13:20

The better part of one's life consists of his friendships.
—Abraham Lincoln

"Okay, I see the problem of my friendless condition, and I understand the principles for meeting my friendship needs. But actually changing my behavior and long-established thinking is quite difficult." Acknowledgment and awareness are the first step to improvement. Before progress can occur, one must believe that a problem exists and that change is possible and needed.

Acting on new knowledge frequently requires, first, the understanding of who we are today; and then, the unlearning, by daily application of biblical principles, of what we previously were taught. To understand ourselves is difficult. Self-examination is a personal and often painful exercise. Plato said, "The unexamined life is not worth living." I think Plato was correct. The work we devote to self-improvement is worth the effort. But there are no shortcuts to personal change and growth. Knowledge and personal examination and often teaming with a few others in the journey provide the foundation for action.

The Bible defines much of life as a process of becoming. We push toward the mark. We grow in grace. We begin as babes in Christ. There are no shortcuts to growth, but the process, getting from where we are to where we want to go, can be enjoyable, although it will take some work.

Assimilating biblical principles takes time. Once a problem is identified, it is the nature of most of us to want an immediate solution. Real change usually takes a while. If we fail to change at the core of our personality, our thinking will not be altered, and our new behavior may just be contrived and wooden. Sooner or later, and more likely sooner, we will backslide and return to old familiar patterns.

You can, however, successfully apply biblical principles and thereby develop quality relationships with others. Sure, it's difficult to look within and ask why we act and think as we do. "Am I selfish?" "Am I a bigot?" "Am I hateful?" "Am I impatient?" "Am I afraid?" "Am I arrogant?" "Am I too comfortable in my self-sufficiency and privacy?" We can ask these and other questions of ourselves, and ponder and even answer them objectively, one by one, in the context of our everyday lives. Some men have sin problems ranging from gambling, porn, sexual harassment, and booze, that get very much in the way of enjoyable and productive relationships with our family members and with friends.

Ingrained Prejudices

I attended a national curriculum and instruction conference at a large university. Methods for educating talented and gifted children were being looked at closely within a school district I was consulting with, and I was quite pleased to learn that this topic was going to be considered at one of the workshop sessions. Arriving a few minutes early, I settled in, anticipating a useful presentation on education of the gifted during this time of

"Common Core" assessment consideration. Sometimes we learn more or differently from what we might have expected.

It turned out that the elementary school teacher who spoke during the session was a well-dressed, young woman. When I learned she was the speaker, my initial thought was, "What could she possibly know about gifted education at the high school and college levels?" However, it was really too late to get up and leave. Besides, it would have been rude, especially since I was on the front row.

I'm glad I remained. She was intelligent and quite informed about the neglected topic of how best to teach academically gifted students. Much of what she said was useful for the levels and type of students I was then interested in learning more about at this conference.

So why was I initially suspect and even turned off before I gave the presenter a chance? I always told my own two children when they were young, "Don't make snap judgments. Give people a chance. Don't be prejudiced." And yet it was I who was prejudiced. Maybe it was because she was young. "What does she know, she's only a kid." Deep down maybe I also held the prejudiced view that an attractive woman got her position because of her appearance. And maybe I reasoned that an elementary school teacher will share little from her background that will be useful or of value to me in my interests and my high school and college responsibilities. Whatever it was that initially I was thinking, clearly my quickly formed, unfair stereotypes were proven wrong.

It is very evident that there remains a "glass ceiling" that hinders women in corporate America. Corporate CEO Sheryl Sandberg is speaking for many when she says in her book, *Lean In: Women, Work, and the Will to Lead*, that while significant progress has been made, we still have a long way to go to reach equality for women in the marketplace.[1]

Many of us could admit that we often make snap judgments about an individual we just met. And then, mentally or physically or both, we withdraw from someone who could become a friend. It might help if we would break the habit of rapidly forming first impressions. If you find you are making quick, categorical conclusions about someone, ask yourself, "Why am I reacting this way toward this person?" Bringing your quickly formed thoughts to a conscious level helps you avoid being unjust.

First impressions, once formed, are rather difficult to change, even when confronted with new information that conflicts with the initial unfair stereotype. We, of course, shouldn't make unfair snap judgments about another person's intelligence, knowledge, character, personality, spirituality, or motives. You may wound another person's spirit or self-confidence and, at the same time, starve yourself from the needed social and spiritual nourishment that comes from involvement with others. The Bible clearly states, for example in James 2, that prejudice is wrong and sinful. It's extremely difficult to uproot ingrained prejudices once established. When we acquire prejudices, we tend unconsciously to defend them even irrationally in the face of facts that contradict our newly formed beliefs.

Discovering my prejudice was only part of what I learned from the teacher who hosted the curriculum workshop. Soon after she began, she divided us into small groups. She wanted us to work together on a project that would help us learn more about teaching gifted students. Well, it did fulfill its intended purpose, but I learned something else as well. The women in our seminar were more eager to work together and to share ideas than the men in the session were willing to do. I honestly felt a little uncomfortable working with others and depending on them to complete the assigned group activity.

Like many men, I am used to working alone. We tend to believe that our greatest successes come from individual and independent efforts on some task. This is changing now that schools have students sometimes work in groups and produce team outcomes. I remember a few occasions in my graduate school experiences when I was put in a situation similar to the workshop for the gifted. My formal learning experiences were largely, however, based on competition with classmates, rather than cooperation.

After I got beyond the uncomfortable feeling in the small group to which I was assigned, I thoroughly enjoyed the learning experience. The adage "If you want a job done right, do it yourself," while often true, is not always true. We need not shrink from social, religious, or work-related activities that bring us into important contact with other people.

Isolation in Moderation

Self-imposed psychological and/or physical isolation is good only in moderation. It's usually less efficient to try to do everything by yourself. The author of the following humorous account is unknown. I'm sure you'll agree that it illustrates our need at times to accept the help of others.

> Dear Sir:
> I am writing in response to your request for more information concerning Block #11 on the insurance form which asks for "cause of injuries" wherein I put "Trying to do the job alone." You said you needed more information, so I trust the following will be sufficient.
> I am a bricklayer by trade, and on the date of injuries I was working alone laying brick around the top of a four-story building when I realized that I had about 500 pounds of brick left over. Rather than carry the bricks down by hand, I decided to put them into a barrel and lower them by a pulley which was fastened to the top of the

building. I secured the end of the rope at ground level and went up to the top of the building and loaded the bricks into the barrel and swung the barrel out with the bricks in it. I then went down and untied the rope, holding it securely to ensure the slow descent of the barrel.

As you will note on Block #6 of the insurance form, I weigh 145 pounds. Due to my shock at being jerked off the ground so swiftly, I lost my presence of mind and forgot to let go of the rope. Between the second and third floors I met the barrel coming down. This accounts for the bruises and lacerations on my upper body.

Regaining my presence of mind again, I held tightly to the rope and proceeded rapidly up the side of the building, not stopping until my right hand was jammed in the pulley. This accounts for the broken thumb.

Despite the pain, I retained my presence of mind and held tightly to the rope. At approximately the same time, however, the barrel of bricks hit the ground and the bottom fell out of the barrel. Devoid of the weight of the bricks, the barrel now weighed about 50 pounds. I again refer you to Block #6 and my weight.

As you would guess, I began a rapid descent. In the vicinity of the second floor I met the barrel coming up. This explains the injuries to my legs and lower body. Slowed only slightly, I continued my descent, landing on the pile of bricks. This accounts for my sprained back and internal injuries.

I am sorry to report, however, that at this point, I again lost my presence of mind and let go of the rope, and as you can imagine, the empty barrel crashed down on me. This accounts for my head injuries.

I trust this answers your concern. Please know that I am finished "trying to do the job alone."

If we would just reach out and ask for help, we could avoid many difficulties and accomplish more in the process. Being a stingy receiver is usually not very helpful for anyone.

Closeness and Intimacy

Andrew M. Greeley, in his book *The Friendship Game*, suggests that fear is the major barrier to friendship. Even within the church we see people sitting in a pew together—alone. We smile, we may even say hello, but we do little else and therefore we don't know one another.

Our behavior at church can be similar to being on an elevator. We don't stand too close to anyone; we don't talk; we look straight ahead; and we can hardly wait for the door to open so we can run out. Being at church can be like one more meeting in the usual Monday through Friday experience. But it should be different. It's Sunday morning. Where are all the men? There are fewer men in the pews. David Murrow, in his book *Why Men Hate Going to Church*, states that many men can be found anywhere but in church. And if they are in church they're not attentive or involved. Church, some say, is boring and full of hypocrites and controlled by women. Men don't feel needed at church, states Murrow, who is very involved with men's ministry activities that are trying to help churches change the culture to responsibly involve men more frequently. Examples of national ministry to men include Iron Sharpens Iron, Forming Connections, Focal Point Ministries, Knights of the 21st Century, Christian Mentors Network, Character That Counts, Authentic Manhood, Men of Honor, Man in the Mirror, Men Stepping Up, Christian

Men's Network, and No Regrets Men's Ministries. In recent years many ministry groups have come together to form the National Coalition of Ministries to Men (NCMM).

Solitary worship is easy, for it demands nothing of us. How does the contemporary church compare with interpersonal relationships that were established by Jesus? In John 13, Jesus says that people will know that we belong to Him if we have love for each other. Over the years, many evangelical leaders have called us to recapture caring, open, sharing relationships together within the body of Christians.

Leaders in this relational type theology movement included Bruce Larson, Keith Miller, Tony Campolo, Larry Crabb, David Moberg, Paul Little, Ken Taylor, Harry Ironside, Os Guinness, and Francis Schaeffer. More recently other evangelicals, including Joel Osteen, David Murrow, Phil Yancey, Rick Warren, Tony Evans, Jim Wallis, and T.D. Jakes continue to express similar calls for meaningful renewal. Usually if something is going to change, then it is up to us to make the change. As the AT&T ad used to say, "Reach out and touch someone." When my son Cameron was in high school, his nationally competitive and very successful marching band had a motto: "If not now, when? If not us, who?"

Before beginning a recent Saturday morning shopping venture, my wife and I had breakfast in a nearby family restaurant. While we were eating, Sue Ann drew my attention to something unusual. Two cars had pulled up to the curb together. A family of five or six piled out of each car. Everyone began talking to each other. There were smiles and handshakes all around. As we were watching what must have been a family reunion, two of the men actually hugged each other unashamedly, and then walked into the restaurant continuing to talk with arms around each other's shoulders.

As we were leaving, I couldn't resist the temptation to find out why these two men were so affectionate. They were glad to talk with me but had not thought much about the display of their feelings. The men were brothers, raised by an affectionate mother who had not instructed her sons to internalize all of their feelings.

Maybe you didn't have such a demonstrative upbringing and you still keep most or all of your feelings to yourself. It's not too late to make some changes. Surely there are several people you care a lot about. Do they know how you feel about them? It's high time you tell them before it might be too late. Some men, due to childhood upbringing, believe they cannot physically show how they feel, especially to another man. Each of us, however, has the ability and the need to tell other people how we feel about them. Of course, we can be discreet, and the time should be appropriate, but the point is, don't let a relationship suffer or die because of poor communication.

When notified that his father was dying in a Los Angeles hospital, a son flew across country to be with his dad. During his vigil at his father's bed, it suddenly struck him that he had never in his entire life told his father he loved him, nor had he hugged him or cried with him at any time in his forty-six years of being his son. He wanted desperately and belatedly to hug and to cry with his dad and to say "I love you, Dad," but his father never regained a fully conscious state. Another lifetime of opportunity was missed, slipped away forever, because of a flawed view of manliness.

I value the relationship I have with my adult son. I want him to know that I love him and always will. I want to show my love for him more consistently. I don't want there to be any doubt in his mind. I used to show my love for him years ago in small ways such as working with him on his go-cart, fishing together at the creek near our home, building a fort in the backyard, building a bunkbed from scratch, making a snowman and snowballs together, and attending Promise Keepers and Stand in the Gap men's ministry events together.

When our son was in fourth grade, his teacher assigned to him and his class a creative writing project. Cameron wrote a paragraph about our father/son relationship that touched my heart and I still have the original short essay framed and on my desk. With his permission, I share it with you:

> I admire my dad. I admire him because he cares for me and loves me. He reads Narnia to me. C.S. Lewis wrote the book. We have lots of laughter and we wonder. My dad and I play football and tag. We built a real fort. It cost about $150. We put shingles on the roof; it didn't have any leaks in it. There were some bugs. My dad is real special to me.

Now that Cameron is a father himself of two very wonderful girls, Ariel and Skylar, my relationship with him has, of course, changed a great deal. Now our time together is spent as two men in simple conversations about a whole host of topics. We don't agree about some stuff, but I think we can talk about anything. He and I have together been attending a men's Bible study group together at his church. We sometimes drive together and talk about all kinds of things. I still do wonder how I can be a better father. I don't feel in any way like a role model, but I'm willing to learn and I view being a father as a very important responsibility even when my "kids" are older. Relationships between fathers and sons are not always close. In fact, physical and emotional estrangement between sons and their fathers is a too common occurrence.

I remember country singer Kenny Rogers talk about the loss of six years in which he failed to even speak to his son Kenny Jr. And President Ronald Reagan's son, Michael, said after his dad died that he had spent his life trying to figure out how to make Ronald Reagan his friend. How much we lose as fathers when we fail to befriend our sons. How much we lose as sons when our fathers fail to befriend us. My own father died when I was only twelve years old. My dad would have wanted to be available for me if he could. I want my adult children to know that as long as I'm alive, and even though we don't agree on everything, I am nevertheless available for them.

We learn much from our fathers about the value and development of male friendships. What did your father teach you? What are you teaching your son or sons?

Be Strong Enough to Cry!

Sue Ann and I were married on a muggy August afternoon in South Bend, Indiana. We had talked about how many children we wanted for our family. Did we want a boy first or a girl? We decided it didn't really matter. Then we discussed how far apart we would space them. If this wasn't naïve enough, we also actually talked about what month we should conceive. If she became pregnant in, say, September, our baby would be born in the spring, which we thought would be an ideal time. Kind of silly, really.

Well, so much for well-intentioned plans. The years came, and the years went. We remained childless, but not for a lack of trying. We saw a urologist and a fertility specialist. Sue Ann took a fertility drug faithfully for three or four years. Still no baby.

We lived in a young married, family-oriented neighborhood. Sue Ann became bored and even a little irritated with the continual conversations about children and birth and labor experiences. And late at night she cried. Her tears expressed her desire for motherhood and our wish to be parents. Being a typical man, I felt uncomfortable when she shared with me her emotions. As I think back, I believe I was actually uncomfortable with my own feelings rather than Sue Ann's. How does a man act? What could I say or do? I guess I wanted to appear strong when I, too, was hurting. We pointed out to God during our innumerable petitions to Him that we had indeed learned the patience that He must obviously intended for us to acquire.

After seeking more medical advice, we agreed (easy for me) that Sue Ann would undergo an operation. We felt the positive result was an answer to prayer. Sue Ann became pregnant a few months following the surgery. It seemed so right. We had been married over seven years, and during those years, we had been involved as church high school youth leaders. All that waiting and frustration were now behind us, or so we thought. It was the middle of the night when Sue Ann woke me up. "Something is wrong. We'd better call 911." The rest of the night and the following two days were spent in the hospital. We lost our child, whom we had grown to love during his nearly six months of development in Sue Ann's body.

I didn't cry. An attending physician told me, "Be strong so you can help your wife. She's emotional right now." But it was me rather than my wife who was acting abnormally. She was expressing her grief and sense of loss in a normal fashion and found it difficult to understand why I didn't cry. I knew the Bible doesn't tell us it is wrong to be full of sorrow. After all, Jesus wept openly and unashamedly at the grave of His friend Lazarus.

I returned home to pack a bag for Sue Ann and make a few phone calls. At home when I was alone I finally cried. Today I know those tears were good for me, for they helped to release the emotional buildup of anger, resentment, and the sense of loss. It would have been better if they had been shared with my wife, but at the time I didn't.

Sue convalesced at home for several days. It was during this time that I was finally able to reveal my emotions by talking and crying with Sue Ann. We planned a week's trip together. This sharing and planning did much to begin the healing of our hearts. I, as much as Sue Ann, needed to talk about what had happened.

I can't remember a story more poignant about the importance of admitting that we must, when appropriate, be prepared to reveal our emotions than this letter from a newspaper column I saved:

> Something happened to me recently that tore me apart. I made my first visit to the Vietnam Memorial looking for Robert Williamson's name. He was my buddy in a unit near Pleiku, where he died in January 1968. The polished marble with all those names and the variety of flowers got to me. I was fighting to keep my composure when I heard someone say "Robert Williamson." In front of me stood a man and a woman with two children. The man was holding up one of the children to touch the name. I wanted to speak to them and find out how they were related. It could have been a meaningful and heartwarming experience, but I was afraid to show my emotions. I knew I would break down and cry, so I walked away. Since then I have relived that incident thousands of times thinking of what I should have done, but of course it's too late.
>
> I realize now that I wouldn't have been the first Vietnam veteran to cry at that monument, and I won't have been the last.
>
> Sincerely, Ken Anderson Oregon, Wisconsin

This American warrior from now over fifty years ago urges each of us to be prepared to show our emotions. He understands now that it is not a sign of weakness. Showing emotion in the right context can reveal strength and self-confidence and can even express concern and fondness for others. We can learn to grieve and to share our grief with others. If we fail to express our emotions, I'm convinced our lives will be lonelier than they need to be and they may possibly also be shortened.

The Necessity of Risk

To share your thoughts, fears, and dreams openly with the crowd is to risk being labeled as naïve or foolish. A reviewer of a book I wrote years ago at one point called me naïve. I think he disagreed with my faith-based worldview. Although as I think about it maybe I *was* a bit naïve. Who knows, but I'll admit I felt irritated by the criticism.

Fear of criticism shouldn't keep us from trying to enter into the lives of others. More than fear of criticism, we should fear loneliness, meaninglessness, and missed opportunities for service to others. Whenever you reach out to another person, you take a chance of being rejected. Leo Buscaglia was a presenter at a conference I attended. I remember him saying, "To love is to risk not being loved in return, but I don't love to be loved in return." Buscaglia was a professor at the University of California who was affectionately sometimes referred to as the "love doctor." He continued, "To hope is to risk despair and to try is to risk failure. But risk must be taken, because the greatest risk in life is to risk nothing. The person who risks nothing, does nothing, has nothing."

Buscaglia is right. A man may avoid suffering and sorrow, but he simply cannot learn and feel and change and grow apart from risk. Chained by his attitudes, he's a slave. He's forfeited his freedom. Only the person who risks is truly free. A sailor takes a risk when he leaves the harbor, but leave the harbor he must.

In a similar spirit, C.S. Lewis wrote:

> To love at all is to be vulnerable. Love anything, and your heart will certainly be wrung and possibly broken. If you want to make sure of keeping

it intact, you must give your heart to no one, not
even to an animal. Wrap it carefully round with
hobbies and little luxuries: avoid all entanglements; lock it up safe in the casket or coffin of
your selfishness. But in that casket—safe, dark,
motionless, airless—it will change. It will not be
broken: instead, it will become unbreakable, im-
penetrable, irredeemable.[2]

What are the personal characteristics of individuals who become millionaires? There have been many studies about the characteristics of millionaires. The findings of most of these studies
may surprise you. You may not be able to predict who is or will
be a millionaire based upon intelligence, education, or even family background. While economically successful people tend to acquire more education and tend to be intelligent, these traits were
not the only predictors of significant wealth. The characteristics
found to be very common among millionaires are:

- They find good in others.
- They have self-confidence.
- They are enthusiastic.
- They appreciate humor.

Each of us can cultivate these relationship useful traits in our
professional and personal lives. To internalize these traits will
make us better individuals, which is certainly more important
than acquiring wealth.

Assessing Yourself

In the next chapter, where we will continue the discussion about
risk taking and goal setting, we will look for ways to identify

those areas of your life that may be hampering your success at making or maintaining top-quality friendships.

Discussion Questions

1. What small steps can you take to begin work on behavioral changes you think are important?

2. How do hugging, crying, or other outward expressions of affection make you feel?

3. In what ways are you like the bricklayer who attempted to do the job alone?

4. What causes prejudice, and what can be done to prevent or remove it? Has prejudice ever hindered you from forming friendships with certain individuals?

CHAPTER 11

Setting Goals for Change

A trip of a thousand miles begins with the first step.
—Chinese proverb

There is nothing on this earth more to be prized than true friends.
—Saint Thomas Aquinas

I don't know how they count our brain cells, but neurosurgeons tell us we have four billion of them. This wonderful, miraculous personal computer in our head is available to help us accomplish our dreams. But even with a great resource like the human brain, we also need the belief that we can succeed in what we take on. In fact, the positive belief in self is the one most significant element in success. Whether you think you can or whether you think you can't, you're probably right.

Track and field fans believed for decades that it was impossible to break the four-minute mile. The human body, no matter how skilled and prepared, could never break this insurmountable barrier, it was thought. But Roger Bannister was confident he could break this physical and psychological barrier. He did so at 3:59.4 minutes in England on May 6, 1954. Soon after the barrier was broken, others followed with marks under four minutes too. They changed their way of thinking of what might actually be possible. Bannister had other goals. He became a neurologist, advanced the science of the nervous system, and was married with four children. He died in 2018 at the age of 88.

In the film *Chariots of Fire*, Eric Liddell is bumped off the track and falls while running in a track competition. He then gets up, runs that much harder—and wins! Do you have the sense of being in a race? Do you have clearly identified goals that give life meaning and push you forward into the future? What goal draws you onward? Significant accomplishments are made by ordinary people with a focused task.

Nehemiah wrote, "Let us start rebuilding" (Nehemiah 2:18). Learning that the remnant of Jews in Judah was in distress and the walls of Jerusalem were broken down, he knew his task was to rebuild the walls of Jerusalem—and he did it. I like that. He had a plan and he worked his plan. Change can occur when we have goals.

We must believe in ourselves and our own potential whether we are encouraged by significant others or not. If you wait around for others to encourage you to action, that encouragement may never come and you may not change. When Walt Disney began to work with animation, he experienced discouragement not only from skeptical bankers but also from his own father. His dad told Walt he ought to "learn a real trade." But Walt Disney believed in himself and his new ideas about fantasy and entertainment. Disney used four words that reveal his confidence and motivation: think, believe, dream, and dare. With little more than a dream, he launched a new industry that has touched millions. The four words that gave him hope can be our words, too, as we work to build more satisfying relationships with other men.

Norman Vincent Peale tells a story that took place in Cincinnati when he was about ten years old. The young Peale and his father were walking on the street when an elderly man in tattered clothing approached, pulled on the boy's sleeve, and said, "Young man, can you give me a dollar?" Dr. Peale remembers that when he shook the man away, it greatly displeased his father. Norman attempted to defend his action with, "But, Dad, he's a bum." His father responded that, "There is no such thing as a bum. There may be some people who haven't made the most of their lives, but all of us are still children of God."

Peale was admonished to go back to the man, give him a dollar, and wish him a Merry Christmas. Quickly he followed his father's instructions. The surprised old man said, "I thank you, young sir. Merry Christmas." Dr. Peale remembers, "In that moment his face became almost beautiful to me. He was no longer a bum." The elderly man had not changed. Rather, Norman had changed. To the young Peale, the man was no longer a bum because Norman, with his father's encouragement, had gotten closer to another person.

A few years ago, newspapers across America reported that a nurse and her two children kept a dead husband and father for eight long years in the bed in which he had died. This true story is so creepy. They changed his linen every few days and attempted to go on with life, pretending he was still alive, perhaps to fraudulently steal the dead man's Social Security income. We, of course, find this gross and beyond bizarre. And yet ordinary people like you and me are often willing to nurse dead ideas, dead religion, dead behavior, and dead values. What would we define as "dead" that we should let go of? What is dead around us that holding us back? We resist change even when God wants us to change, even when we know in our heads and our hearts it's in our best interest to change.

Facing Our Fears

During the Great Depression, President Franklin D Roosevelt said, "The only thing we have to fear is fear itself." Our fears, often unconscious, tend to paralyze us, preventing the possibility of change. "God hath not given us the spirit of fear but... of a sound mind" (2 Timothy 1:7 KJV). We have, therefore, the ability to deal with our fears rationally, logically, and prayerfully as we lean on the support of God and those who love us. Fear, squarely faced, tends to ebb in significance. In John Bunyan's seventeenth-century classic *Pilgrim's Progress*, Christian's path was beset by alarming shapes that scuttled about in the shifting mists. These sinister monsters proved to be tiny creatures unable to hurt anyone. Your fears and my fears may be unnecessary and simply a waste of time and energy. I'll attempt a paraphrase of Philippians 4:6: "Don't be uptight about this. Rather, ask God to help you with your fears." It is useful to remind ourselves from time to time that we have not been given a spirit of fear.

Years ago, papers and magazines across America told the story of Shoichi Yokoi, a World War II Japanese soldier. For twenty-eight years following the war, Shoichi Yokoi lived as a hermit in a cave on the island of Guam. He and several like him ignored pamphlets dropped from planes that announced the end of the war. Rather than take the risk of possible imprisonment, he chose to live in a self-imposed prison of his own making and thus gave up years of freedom. He died in 2014. We find this hard to believe, and yet many of us men live in caves of emotionlessness and lack of intimacy and enjoyment and sharing with others that is largely self-inflicted.

If we are to break out of our very private world, we must break through to other men in short, small stages. As we do, our fears will ebb. Ask opinions of others and be willing to share a few of your own. By asking their thoughts on a topic, you send out the subtle message that you recognize and respect them as individuals. William James, the influential psychologist of the early 1900s, said, "The deepest principle of man is the craving to be appreciated." And we never outgrow our need to be appreciated.

When I was teaching high school and college social science and history classes, I required students to prepare a research paper on a problem or issue in American society. Part of the assignment was to interview two individuals who were directly involved in some way with the subject matter of the paper. To be sure, this assignment was not often received with enthusiasm. Students feared that the men and women they wanted to interview would resent giving them the proper time or attention. These students were also afraid they would ask dumb questions of those being interviewed.

We discovered that, with few exceptions, those interviewed were very willing to talk with students. Some of them even called me to offer to speak to the entire class or just to say thanks for the opportunity to share. They were glad to take the time to share because someone asked their opinion about some topic that was important to them. The students sent thank-you notes and reported enthusiastically that it was a good experience. Similar to these students, we need to ask questions and take an interest in others. Fear is unnecessary. Reach out. Usually you'll be pleasantly surprised with the good connections you'll experience.

You Really Can Change!

Asking in prayer for God's help along with your own resolve provides the best combination for change known to man. Your own inner strength is more powerful than you might at first realize. God has given each of us various gifts and talents that He intends for us to use. D. L. Moody once said that, "If your house is burning, at that moment don't pray about it; just get up and put the fire out." It has been said that some Christians act so heavenly they are of no earthly good. It is not a contradiction to depend upon God and yourself at the same time. You realize that God is the ultimate source of your strength and at the same time, that you are personally responsible for what you do and say.

You must believe in yourself and in your ability to change. Don't meditate on past defeats. Even in areas of your life where you have experienced failure, the correct response is not "I can't do this." With this attitude you'll never be able to do whatever "this" might be. A more appropriate and useful response is, "With God's help, I'll work hard to turn this past failure into victory" or "I haven't yet but I'm working on it." In the book *How to Be Your Own Best Friend*, the authors suggest, "If we all just kept on doing exactly what we've done up to now, people would never change, and people are changing all the time." That's growth, doing what you've never done before.

In my desk at home, I have a card that reads, "You Are What You Do, Not What You Say You'll Do." This reminder helps me somehow with one of my persistent weaknesses—impatience. A friend told me I should ask God for patience and I should tell Him I want it right now. That was his attempt at humor. But the point is, it is not enough for me to say I'd like to be a more patient person. I need to convert the platitude into action, where I actually show and live a more patient life. What roadblocks in your life are preventing you from fully participating in a more useful, abundant life? What patterns of thought or behavior now separate you from applying biblical principles of friendship?

One secret of success in changing long-standing patterns is first to concentrate on specific items that need change and second, to strive for small improvements. The trip of a thousand miles begins with a single step. Begin small. As you create and achieve realistic short-range goals, sooner or later you'll enjoy significant improvements.

What now prevents you from making biblical principles and positive personality traits part of your life? What are the front burner issues that you're concerned about? You can focus on these areas. Ask yourself, why this problem? Where am I right now with this issue? What is my goal? And how do I get from where I am to where I want to be? Set goals for yourself. Write them down and list in small, manageable incremental steps how you'll accomplish the eventual desired end result.

In the final analysis, you cannot say that you are what you are because society has taught you to be macho, or because your parents raised you incorrectly, or because you were unduly influenced either too early or too late in life, or because you're a man, or because of any other external factor. To allow yourself to be controlled by external factors is to become something like a robot. You are what you are because you have chosen to be what you are. You are the person in control of your life. God has given to us free will whereby we can make good or poor decisions. You may use the free will and ability you have to seek God's wisdom and influence in your life as you seek His will for the rest of your life.

The Freudians and other social determinists have given us some insights into the human mind, but they err on at least one critical point. You and I are responsible to God and our fellow humans for our behavior because we are relatively free to discern and to behave much as we please. It was reported that a gang of New York teenagers nearly killed a jogger in Central Park because "they felt like it." One New York columnist blamed society for the vicious attack rather than the teenagers themselves. Many columnists, including George Will, fired back that to blame society was nonsense. If we are to remain civilized, individuals must be responsible and held responsible for their own behavior, circumstances notwithstanding. We are not puppets on strings, totally controlled by social and psychological forces beyond our control.

Edward O. Wilson, in his controversial book *Social Biology*, would disagree. He claims that our behavior is the result of how we were raised and how our genes were programmed. In virtually every field of social science today, and now also in the natural sciences, mankind is viewed as a manipulated machine incapable of independent decision-making. Such a controlled human, of course, is not responsible for his own behavior and is useful only if he can produce something valued by the culture. Such programmed humans are disposable and lack morals or intrinsic value.

This is not the Bible's view of man. We are not a *tabula rasa* or a mindless lump of clay to be molded by others or by biological genes. How much control do I really have over my own life? Can I change on my own, or do I need counseling to improve my patterns of living? In some cases, we can engage in self-examination on a solo basis. Self-reflection and contemplation can be helpful, but many people need the added insights, understanding, and objectivity that can be provided only by an outsider such as a close friend, wife, minister, or counselor.

When I mention therapy, what comes to your mind? Some Christians shun the term, associating it with Freudian psychology and psychoanalysis. John Montgomery says we should be morally offended by Sigmund Freud's explaining God away as a mythical father figure. Christians rather should explain Freud away as a product of his own neurosis. Freud had serious emotional problems himself, as did his disciple Carl Jung, who admitted he had little interest in helping suffering humanity, only in understanding it. Accepting without critical examination the tenets of modern psychology as practiced by some may not be a good idea. Modern psychiatry is less Freudian and less determinist and less behaviorally oriented than its twentieth-century version, and it can possibly be found helpful to those who are discerning.

Where can we find counseling help if we reject some of the tenets of psychoanalysis? After all, emotional pain is a real phenomenon. Fortunately, many emotional problems can be helped if those who are suffering know that someone really cares about them. O. Quentin Hyder, M.D., writes:

> This is the key to good psychology and counseling—to care, to really care, and to let the sufferer know that you care. If more Christians made themselves available in this way to help the weaker brother and sister in need when the troubles

first started, there would be far fewer numbers of them having to go later for professional help. The burden of my message is that caring Christians can significantly contribute to the mental and emotional health of their fellow church members and Christian friends. To do so we must make ourselves available and give time and our own emotional energies and resources to succor those in need.[1]

People with concerning adjustment problems can consult with a trusted counselor or professional psychologist. Professional counselors usually have graduate school degrees and are licensed by the state where they serve. If medication is needed, psychiatrists are the ones who are licensed to evaluate a patient's need for medicine and to grant prescriptions. In some cases, you can change positively without the use of professional help, but it is of great value to have a trusted and concerned individual, whatever their background, who cares about you to talk with.

In other cases, such as with depression and some addictions, professional help will likely be a necessity. Professional help can be a resource that God has made available. The Scripture states that when you seek Him, God can free you from your old negative lifestyle patterns (2 Corinthians 5:17) and provide you with what is good for both you and those around you (Galatians 5:22–23; 2 Peter 1:5–7). With God's help and with perhaps the listening ear of a trusted friend, many people can introduce positive changes into their lives.

Our greatest problem is not other people but rather ourselves. Remember the Pogo quote at the beginning of Chapter 3? "We have met the enemy and he is us." Former president Jimmy Carter says that his faith has given him, at least most of the time, "... a realization that it is my own fault if I feel lonely, alienated, unhappy, frustrated, inadequate, bereft of purpose, or afraid. This tends to prevent my blaming other people for my own problems."[2] We can be and often are our own worst enemy. In the Galatians letter (5:17), Paul records that for the Christian, our human nature and our spiritual natures are in dire conflict. Good intentions, no matter how pure, like New Year's resolutions, rarely result in long-term changed attitudes and behavior. You need your own resolve and dedication to be sure, but one additional step is also needed. Without the support of God and the love of friends and family, positive changes, if they occur at all, are usually cosmetic and short-lived.

"Let God change you inwardly" (Romans 12:2 TEV). J.B. Phillips translates this verse, "Let God remold your minds from within." The next chapter will introduce several ways to assist with our journey to continue to make positive, long-lasting changes.

Discussion Questions

1. Create three realistic short-term, positive and measurable goals for yourself. Write them down along with specific steps and resources needed to help you reach your goals.

2. What are the barriers that could block your progress toward accomplishing these goals? How can the identified roadblocks best be minimized or overcome?

3. Why do we resist positive change, even when we know it is in our best interest? What can you do to reduce your fears of change and fears of rejection?

4. To what degree are we really responsible for our own individual actions and thoughts?

CHAPTER 12

Confronting American Culture

*Do not conform any longer to the pattern of this world but be
transformed by the renewing of your mind. Then you will be
able to test and approve what God's will is.*
—Romans 12:2

*Whatsoever things are true, honorable, just, pure, lovely,
gracious, excellent, praiseworthy, think on these things.*
—Philippians 4:8

During the nineteenth century, the United States was
mainly a rural and agricultural nation. Most families
lived on farms in sparsely populated areas. Work and
other activities were done together by all members of the family. The wife, husband, and children all shared the tasks of producing what the family itself consumed.

As the country developed into an industrial nation, gender
roles became more specialized and rigid. Usually it was the man
who left the home and the farm to earn a living in town. Children
left home to attend school. Women remained in the home to care
for small children and household duties. The gender roles became more specifically defined. But during World War II, hundreds of thousands of American women left home to enter the
factories in an attempt to help with the war effort.

Following the war, for economic and social reasons, many
women remained in the workforce, and many got married. Classes

were full as many men went to college on the GI Bill. With wives working full-time and husbands at work and in school, less of a stigma existed for men who shared domestic chores of laundry, shopping, and cleaning. Our culture began to change its definition again of male or female behavior. But even with the many changes in gender roles, we still have not yet redefined maleness to the extent that men can express their feelings and fears and be able to ask for help in certain situations.

Frontier Ethic

Despite the significant changes in the twentieth and now the twenty-first century, many men still adhere to what might be called a frontier ethic, a throwback to the eighteenth and nineteenth centuries. These earlier times remind us of the image of the powerful autonomous men of the Wild West. In the shootout at the OK Corral, one could not afford to be second best. On the frontier combating the elements, including starvation, disease, wild animals, and Indians, a man had to win. First place was often all that was available. To lose or to come in second place was to die.

While the frontier disappeared well over a century ago, many still cling to a frontier mentality. The frontier behavior and thinking that served earlier generations in their struggles with physical survival is an anachronism today. We still feel that finishing first is vital to our masculinity and to our emotional survival. During the 1970s, the Minnesota Vikings won many football playoff championships but were relegated by the press to the loser category since they failed to win the "big one." The big one, of course, is the Super Bowl, America's most important annual pageant.

The San Francisco Giants got the same treatment in the late 1950s and 1960s. The Dallas Cowboys also had a great string of playoff victories in the 1960s. What was said of these winning teams? They, too, couldn't win the big one. So far in the new twenty-first century only one team, the New England Patriots in 2004 and 2005, accomplished back-to-back Super Bowl victories. For the record, the Patriots also won in 2015 and 2017 and were back in the Super Bowl in 2018, which was won for the first time by the Philadelphia Eagles. Denver won in 2016. The Patriots won their sixth Super Bowl in 2019 with a 13 to 3 score against the Los Angeles Rams. Some say that heated competition makes winners, and so it does or so it can. But it makes dozens more non-winners if the only acceptable standard is to win the so-called big one.

I have been a Chicago Cubs fan from birth. As a "north sider" I could hardly be anything else. I'm sure the whole world knows the Chicago Cubs won their second World Series in 2016. The first time they did so was in 1908. Many of us wished for the Cubs to win the World Series the next year, but they did not repeat in 2017, and in 2018 the Cubs lost their division race to the Milwaukee Brewers. Back-to-back super wins are quite rare at any level in any sport.

Every athlete should do his or her best. Former Dodger pitcher Orel Hershiser says in his book *Out of the Blue* that as a Christian and as a man, he is obligated to do the best he can do. To do otherwise would be hypocrisy or passive acceptance of defeat. High standards and devotion to a task are important, but they are not to be confused with winning at any cost or assuming that losing a contest makes one a failure. Unfortunately, we tend to place a high value on winners.

Neil Armstrong was the first man on the moon. Why don't we know who was second? Who were the vice presidents in the administrations of Washington, Jefferson, Lincoln, Wilson, Roosevelt, Kennedy, Nixon, or Carter? Even in more recent years, many would be hard-pressed to identify the vice presidents in the Bush #41, Clinton, Bush #43, Obama, or Trump administrations. Is this because we just view the vice president as "second place"? We're told, although incorrectly, that Columbus was first to discover America. Who was said to be second? The second person to fly solo across the Atlantic was nearly as daring as Charles Lindbergh, but no one ever hears of him or her.

Might makes right today as well as it did on the frontier. Money and power made even a sleazy character like Al Capone important. The frontier ethic of being first at all costs is only one anachronistic legacy that still plagues our culture's view of the way men should perform in the twenty-first century.

Social Darwinism

In the 1880s, a new philosophy was popularized, partially to justify an emerging ruthlessness in business, but also to explain why only a few were "winners" in the competitive game of life. Those with great wealth might have needed some way philosophically to lessen the guilt and concern they may have felt when they surveyed the desperate poverty endured by multitudes. The extremely rich oil tycoon Nelson Rockefeller was once asked how much money is enough. Rockefeller answered, "Just a little bit more."

Rather than attempt to reform the economic system to make it more benevolent, many of the rich sought a system or philosophy to explain why the poor were poor and had only themselves to blame for their own poverty. Using the biological theories developed by Charles Darwin and published in 1859 in his book the *Origin of Species*, the English philosopher Herbert Spencer, and others, developed the idea of Social Darwinism. The disparity of the very rich and the very poor was the result of the iron laws of nature, Spencer argued. The rich, and many of the poor themselves, believed Spencer's explanation that fixed laws of nature existed to guide human conduct. Nature was vicious, not beneficent, and survival of the fittest was the law for human behavior as well as for human and animal biology. The poor and handicapped were viewed by some as unfit and expendable since nature was attempting to better each species.

Therefore, if you had great wealth, it was not due to luck or a gift from your parents or from God, but rather because you were superior to other creatures and were meant to lord it over lesser men as some powerful animals control or destroy their prey. Natural selection, not divine providence, reigned supreme. Many scoffed when Robert Bly wrote the bestseller *Iron John* about fierce masculinity and brought men together for male bonding at Wild Man gatherings around America, where he called out to men to stop being "good little boys." He went on to say that at times you must say "no way" to women, and take control, stand up for yourself, and overcome the estranged relationship you have with fathers who withheld their acceptance and love. He'd have men stomp around a firepit at night retreat sessions, where he encouraged them to become masters and take control of their lives. Critics say of Bly that he wants men to be self-centered savages.

There exists a predatory thinking that has affected the American male psyche, and many have drifted away from the Christian worldview, which, as illustrated in Jesus, elevates the values of gentleness, concern, and sensitivity for others. Rather than undermine or explain away the weak, Jesus was compassionate and offered help. His discussion of the Good Samaritan will forever stand as a beacon of hope for the downtrodden and also as a challenge for those who have the capacity to reach out to the less fortunate. Jesus came to serve others (Matthew 20:28). Jesus had time for people, even so-called unimportant people like the woman at the well. He touched people like the leper (Luke 5:12–13), and He wasn't too concerned if others thought He was doing the wrong thing according to the cultural norms of the time. And He wanted to spend time with children (Mark 10:13–16). These several characteristics are not exactly highly valued or practiced widely today in our contemporary culture.

Author Horatio Alger perpetuated the myth of the self-made and completely self-reliant man in his widely read novels from the nineteenth century. Unfortunately for the multitudes who don't finish first, who never become corporate presidents or champions in their fields, they are left with feelings of failure. Ironically perhaps, Alger himself is an example of the failure to live up to the American dream, as his own life did not turn out well. What is not mentioned in his novels is that men with power and money tend to pass on their money and power to their children. And children of poor parents tend to produce children who grow up poor despite effort and a desire by many to rise above their economic conditions.

This is, thankfully, not always true, especially in America, where educational and economic opportunities really do exist. We know that America historically has maintained a middle class that includes the children and grandchildren and great-grandchildren of lower classes that migrated to America through several centuries, including the twenty-first century. Many progressives at the beginning of the twentieth century, President Theodore Roosevelt among them, worked to reduce the inordinate influence of the super-rich and corrupt politicians. Following the worst economic downturn since the Great Depression, the Great Recession of 2008 has resulted in more economic disparity among Americans and a shrinking of the middle class and private sector labor union membership. While unemployment numbers have lessened recently, underemployment numbers have remained stubbornly elevated.

A few people began to challenge the cultural illusion of Social Darwinism during the Great Depression, when both very able and very willing men were unable to find work of any sort, much less the great jobs associated with money and power. They were not the sole determiners of their destiny. Impersonal enemies, such as economic conditions and the lack of available jobs, prevented many people from being fully self-reliant. My German great-grandmother used to talk about the 1930s and the hungry, out-of-work men who would on occasion knock at her front door on the north side of Chicago and ask for a piece of bread or a sandwich.

In Psalm 147, using symbols of physical strength, David illustrates how the LORD is not impressed with the autonomous myth of human strength that is ingrained in our culture. David records, "He does not delight in the strength of the horse; He takes no pleasure in the legs of a man. The LORD takes pleasure in those who fear Him, in those who hope in His mercy" (Psalm 147:10–11). David is telling us not to depend solely upon ourselves for strength. He says, "The LORD God is my strength and my shield" (Psalm 28:7).

American men have varying degrees of difficulty turning to another person or to God for strength in a time of need. It goes against the grain of our way of thinking. Motivational speaker Greg Risberg once said that John Wayne, who in the minds of many embodied the ideal man, both on and off the screen, wouldn't say, "I'm scared, let's think about this." Rather he would only say, "Let's kill the SOBs."

In our way forward, we can search the Scriptures and the life of Christ for better masculine lifestyle examples of how to live in our world. We need to act and think in a manner that is consistent with our faith and values. We are not called to be odd or reactionary. Rather we are called to be caring and compassionate.

Signs of Civilization

When I was a teacher, I might ask students to define an advanced civilization. Many students would mention countries or cultures that had achieved a technological superiority over their contemporaries. Like most people, the students invariably associated technological advancement as an indication of higher civilization. Most often mentioned was America's ability to conduct a successful moon landing in July 1969. Even the Quaker president of the United States at the time, Richard Nixon, referred to the lunar landing as "the greatest event in all of world history," therefore, I suppose, superseding the creation of the world, the fall of man, the flood, the birth, death, and resurrection of Jesus Christ, the formation of democracies, the invention of vaccinations, and the discovery of the cures of many diseases. The moon landing was a mechanical triumph of the highest order, but what of our triumphs in the spiritual and human realms?

The advance of technology has been a mixed blessing. Technology may oddly actually cut down the time we spend with loved ones. People watch television at night now, while in earlier times people talked and played games together with family members and neighbors. And now many are spending much of their time with a growing variety of smart devices and in social media interaction. At a Panera Bread restaurant last weekend, I saw six college-age students sitting around the same lunch table. Each was on their own iPad or iPhone, and they were not speaking for long periods to each other or even looking at each other. I'm not sure the smart devices have added all that much quality to our lives and sense of togetherness. In 2 Corinthians 4:18, we read about the inadequacy of material things: "We do not look at the things which are seen, but at the things which are not seen. For the things which are seen are temporary, but the things which are not seen are eternal."

The mark of civilization is not material or technological advancement. Nazi Germany in the 1930s and early 1940s silenced the message of Christ and Judaism while killing millions of people efficiently and rapidly with some of the most sophisticated technology of those decades; and yet by anyone's definition the Nazis must be viewed as barbaric, inhuman, and uncivilized.

Armed communist Bolsheviks seized the Winter Palace in Petrograd in 1917 in the city that is now St. Petersburg. David Satter says that the Bolshevik plague, which began in Russia, was the greatest catastrophe in human history. The result of 100 years of communism was 100 million people dead. It is incomprehensible the cost in human suffering and death caused by atheistic communism. Satter tells us, "If there is one lesson the communist century should have taught, it is that the independent authority of universal moral principles cannot be an afterthought, since it is the conviction on which all of civilization depends."[1]

The twentieth century was horrific, the worst in all of recorded history in the terms of the slaughter of military personnel and civilians alike by many governments especially those of Japan, Germany, China, and the Soviet Union. These and other nations abandoned biblical principles of morality, including the worth and dignity of every individual, and in the resulting moral vacuum adopted the extreme doctrines of fascism and communism. In biblically oriented societies, there exists the belief that the state exists to serve the people. With fascism and communism and other anti-biblical economic and social philosophies, the resulting view is that the people serve the state. Tragedy results when individuals and nations turn away from God. Morality and the rule of law and the conviction that the state exists for and by the people are essential moral values inherent in our civilization and are found in the Bible. The bedrock essential resource for our laws, morals, and values is the Bible.

The measure of civilization, I told my students, is how individuals and an entire culture treat each other, especially how individuals treat the weak, those less fortunate who lack power and influence. The weak are often the defenseless, those who lack strength in body, mind, or spirit. Men are not meant to dominate these people, but they are to emulate the servant's heart of Jesus. In the nineteenth and early twentieth centuries, the Christian community, not the Social Darwinists, worked for the removal of slavery, exploitive child labor practices, predatory sexual abuse, inhumane prisons, elder abuse, and primitive mental institutions.

Romans 14 and 15 call for us to be active in our communities. We are to be involved in helping those who have real needs, which they themselves are unable to satisfy. Deuteronomy 15:7–8 reads, "If there is among you a poor man you shall open your hand to him and lend him sufficient for his need" (RSV). We should be involved in our communities all of the time, not just when we are upset about something. There is a serious lack of Christian influence and involvement, especially with leadership positions in every sector of our communities. In business, education, government, and every aspect of our communities, we are not called to be parochial; rather we are called to be involved. First Timothy 6:18 instructs us "to do good, to be rich in good deeds, and to be generous and willing to share."

Late in the nineteenth century, Ferdinand Tönnies, a German sociologist, contrasted and generalized two distinct kinds of societies. One is *gemeinschaft*, which means commitment to community, sense of belonging, moral stability, tradition, sharing of attitudes, intimacy and extended kinship, fixed status, and shared sacred values. In contrast, *gesellschaft* loosely translates as a group created for a special purpose, like a business established to pursue a self-interest. People freely join this type of society and see it as a practical way of achieving certain goals. American men fit best with this kind of group. They learn early in life that they are to concentrate on pursuing their own goals and not be too connected to or concerned with relationships and concerns of other work associates and acquaintances.

If given the conscious choice of either freedom and convenience or community and intimacy, it would be difficult for most of us to choose. We enjoy our privacy even though we know and have awareness that solitude can contribute to loneliness.

Ralph Keyes, author of *We, the Lonely People*, says that above all else Americans value mobility, privacy, and convenience. And it is these very traits that are the source of our lack of community and our loneliness. Of these three, privacy is our most cherished value. But it has not always been this way. Keyes reminds us, "Privacy as an ideal, even as a concept, is relatively modern. Marshall McLuhan says it took the invention of print to tear man from his tribes and plant the dream of individualism and isolation in his brain. Historian Jacob Burchardt says that before the Renaissance, Western man was barely aware of himself as an individual. Mostly he drew identity from membership in groups—family, tribe, church, guild."[2]

We have a desire to be left alone. We don't associate being alone with loneliness. We are a private people. In recent generations we have been able to become self-sufficient as individuals. We don't need other people as previous generations did to get through life on a day-to-day basis. The introduction of time and labor-saving technology has reduced our dependence upon others to respond to daily problems. Nebraska U.S. Senator Ben Sasse in his book *The Vanishing American Adult* said in 2018 that we have an American crisis of loneliness and social disconnection that will impact negatively our country.

What can we do? We can introduce biblical principles into our culture where we live and work and expect to see good things happen. Our offer of friendships, our opening up to others, can be an important solace at a time when traditional institutions are in a state of flux and possibly decline. Marriage, community, and in many cases, the church no longer provide the degree of influence and predictable intimacy experienced in earlier generations. In his 2018 book, *One in Christ*, pastor David Ireland says we must go into all parts of our individual worlds and therefore become racially and culturally accommodating, true reconcilers who labor to make genuine relationships and to bring people together in Christ. To begin to seriously confront the macho, non-biblical male values of our culture, it will be helpful to consider a cross-cultural masculinity that is based upon Scripture.

Biblical Masculinity

We could benefit from a broader definition of what it means to be masculine in our American culture. Rather than spend much of our time criticizing non-biblical, macho lifestyles, we can go positively on the offensive by providing our family, friends, and coworkers a masculinity that conforms to biblical principles.

Many in our communities are alone and lonely. People long for connectedness and commitment. The "me first" strategy is losing appeal with this millennial cohort generation, born between 1982 and 2004, as people hunger for deeper, more sustained, committed relationships. Maybe in our time, in our generation, we can produce a new "We Generation."

Social scientists such as Thorstein Veblen, Margaret Mead, Vance Packard, David Reisman, Alvin Toffler, Peter Berger, Suzanne Gordon, Ralph Keyes, C. W. Mills, and Erich Fromm informed us throughout much of the twentieth century with their research and in their several influential books that we are living in a culture that is both materialist and consumption-oriented that produces selfish and lonely individuals. Men possess a materialistic view of the world. They view women as sex objects and other men as objects to be manipulated toward their own selfish economic ends. This troubling view of both men and women is belatedly on display without embarrassment or concern, even at the highest levels of our national government.

Christians should work to liberate men from destructive definitions of masculinity that prevent the development of healthy interpersonal relationships. Call this a man's liberation movement if you like. The fact is men in the United States and other countries need to change. Committed Christians can be influential in the lives of other Americans as we strive to live daily a masculinity that is biblical.

To be truly masculine is to be a follower and imitator of Jesus Christ. Jesus is our great example (1 Peter 2:21). Commenting on this fundamental truth, Gary Collins lists several Christlike characteristics that we can study and learn from and use as a guide for our behavior and thoughts each day. Christ was:

1. Dependent on God for daily guidance, frequently at prayer, and thoroughly familiar with the Scriptures.
2. Intolerant of sin and a firm defender of justice.
3. Compassionate and not afraid to show His feelings.
4. Knowledgeable of events around Him, concerned about the poor and needy, helpful in alleviating suffering, sensitive to others, and willing to tolerate personality differences.
5. Characterized by love, joy, peace, patience, kindness, goodness, faithfulness, gentleness, and self-control.3

Men who emulate Jesus as their example for masculinity affirm that they are able to be warm, loving, caring, open, sensitive human beings. This masculinity rejects the narrow, rigid, traditional, and often destructive manly role that demands that we be tough, aggressive, and unfeeling. Christlike masculinity puts into practice both the biblical principles of friendship from Chapter 6 and the personality traits discussed in Chapter 7.

God's ways are not our ways or our culture's ways. Writing over two centuries ago and referring to the United States, the French visitor to America, Alexis de Tocqueville, observed, "I know of no country, indeed, where the love of money has taken a stronger hold on the affections of men." The young urban professionals of the 1990s and even today's twenty- or thirty-something millennials are maintaining the accuracy of the de Tocqueville observation of American culture.

Many materialists are climbing a success ladder that leads to nowhere. Leonardo DiCaprio's character in the 2014 movie, *The Wolf of Wall Street* reminds me of this kind of guy. In Luke 16:19–31 Jesus tells a parable about a man who, like many today, accumulated both wealth and power. In our culture we would call him a success, even though he was selfish and had no concern for the beggar Lazarus at his gate. Moreover, he paid the ultimate cost for his "success." He ended up in Hades, while Lazarus, a, failure on the basis of our culture's standards, went to be with God.

The application of biblical knowledge and principles can not only change your life and the lives of those around you, but it also can extend to the larger culture. It seems to me that we are largely missing a golden opportunity in this generation to really help individuals see the bankruptcy of contemporary self-centered culture.

What is highly valued within our culture may well be detestable to God (Luke 16:15), but not because He doesn't want us to enjoy life. On the contrary, the Bible teaches that God wants us to live life to the fullest. To accomplish this, we must live within and in accordance with certain given physical, psychological, and moral laws or principles—all given to us by God in the Bible.

What we perceive "through a glass darkly" (1 Corinthians 13:12 KJV) to be gold, silver, and precious stones may actually be wood, hay, and stubble. To positively influence the lives of others at this time in our nation's history, we should be able to distinguish between our culture's values and the values we discover in the Bible. Vernon C. Grounds, former president of Conservative Baptist Seminary in Denver, reminds us that successful people in history like Jesus, Paul, Peter, and Stephen were usually in conflict with their culture. Our culture has little time for the criteria God has established for us in our dealings with others. God's measure of a man is Christlike love (1 Corinthians 13:1–3), which produces a servant's heart and behavior (Matthew. 20:25–27). But this is a far cry from the ingrained mental images of masculinity we have perpetuated in our culture.

A servant's heart should not be equated with a milquetoast Christian timid acquiescence to our culture. At a meeting I heard a man say, "I'll admit I'm a Christian, but I feel that pornography is wrong." Admit? Admit what? The poor fellow was defensive and nervous as he attempted to articulate his faith while apologizing for it all in the same sentence. Which is worse, an anemic, half-hearted comment or no comment at all? I think silence is even worse than a weak-willed attempted defense of the biblical worldview. Even though our beliefs may be in the minority, we need not be apologetic. In any event, you don't determine what is true or right by a head count or by who has the loudest voice. Between the extremes of a weak-willed spirit and a harsh arrogance lies a calm, informed confidence that is the better road to travel.

What can you do in a practical and positive way to influence the culture you live in? Each of us can evaluate our own thinking and behaving, making sure we are part of the solution rather than part of the problem. We can begin with the culture of our home, then our church, and then our community. Following are a few ideas to help us evaluate our influence in these three important areas of our daily lives.

Home and Family

Traditional cultural images of masculinity have treated women as objects to be manipulated, ignored, patronized, or in other ways not taken seriously. Macho men are rarely respected by emotionally well-adjusted women. For a man to cling to a macho attitude is both insensitive and immature from a biblical perspective and is just plain dumb, especially if you want to get along with the women in your life. The Bible indicates that a man should be focused upon the needs of others. And if you are married, you should love and care for your wife as you do yourself (Ephesians 5:28, 33).

The National Center for Health Statistics published an encouraging report in 2014. It seems that more dads are "doing diapers" and are not too busy to bathe, dress, and play with their own young children. Hands-on fathering is apparently becoming more commonplace. More involved dads are producing better-adjusted children. Isn't this a rather obvious outcome with more involved dads? It is no surprise that when husbands share parenting and domestic responsibilities, it contributes significantly and directly to better and more loving marriages, according to the NCHS survey report.4 The women of America have said for generations that involved dads make for happier, less exhausted wives and therefore better marriages. They didn't need some federal report to confirm what they have always known. Hopefully this is a trend that will continue and grow.

The apostle Peter tells husbands that they should give honor to their wives and share everything with them (1 Peter 3:7–11). While no one knows for sure, Peter may have written this section of Scripture after he had an argument with his wife. Imagine the following situation: Peter comes home after a full day of fishing or ministry with Jesus. Instead of asking his wife about her day, he says in a matter-of-fact manner, "What's for dinner; when do we eat?" Learning that they will have fish for dinner in a few minutes, he blurts out, "What? Fish again?" Or perhaps she wanted to talk with him about something or nothing in particular and he didn't listen, or he listened only half-heartedly.

Following a typical day caring for children, washing the clothes at the river, and cooking the evening meal, Peter's wife wasn't prepared for or interested in his insensitivity and being taken for granted. She may have been unhappy and perhaps left the room. Feeling sorry for himself, Peter may have decided to pray, "What's wrong with her? I don't understand her sometimes. I try to be a good husband." Peter's prayer doesn't get any higher than his family room ceiling. About this time, the Spirit of God may have given him verse 7 of 1 Peter 3, which told him, and tells us, that if a husband doesn't live with his wife in a respectful, loving way, his prayers will be virtually worthless.

Prayer cannot be used as a substitute for obedience. Realizing his mistake, Peter could have gone to his wife, and said and meant those two difficult words, "I'm sorry." And even though his need to say "I'm sorry" had happened several times before and she knew it would likely occur in the future, she nevertheless was gracious and forgiving and accepted his apology. Only after his reconciliation with his wife was Peter able to communicate again with God. Perhaps to summarize the lesson he had just learned, the Spirit of God gave to Peter verse 8: "Finally, all of you, live in harmony with one another; be sympathetic, love as brothers, be compassionate and humble."

Of course, a man doesn't have to be either a husband or a father to exercise biblical masculinity. Jesus never married and, possibly, neither did Paul, yet both were exemplary masculine personalities. In addition to husband and father, a man may have the privilege and responsibility within a family to be an uncle, godparent, brother, nephew, grandfather, cousin, and friend. Married or not, parent or not, the biblical masculine man treats women and children and other men all the same way, with love and respect.

In the Church

I remember asking the members of my adult elective Sunday school class what they as individuals could do to befriend both the new and established members of our church. Their comments were interesting. "Welcome the new people with a smile and a handshake"; "Be hospitable"; "Invite new people to your home or a restaurant for coffee or lunch following the service"; "The important thing is not to be pushy but to be available." All agreed that a new or established person's race, educational level, or income should not matter.

A class member said that with established church people, "We should be available in time of need, not overbearing but be there if needed." Another man, a deacon, said, "We should be sensitive and available for people who are lonely or troubled somehow or experiencing some fellowship need."

We had a good class discussion, but in reality, it is hard to change the current climate and make real and positive changes. Our churches, like other institutions, are affected by the impersonality of our culture. Most cult experts agree that some people turn to cults and outwardly very friendly sects because they provide at least the appearance of emotional support and love, which is lacking in many mainline and evangelical churches.

Often our principal contact in a new church is with an official greeter, dutifully commissioned and recognizable by his or her carnation or ribbon or place to stand. It is an assigned official duty to be nice and to greet people. The other church members sit alone or with their own group or family and rarely venture forth to meet new people. In one evangelical church, a friend of mine who attended for several weeks was told that visitors should meet at a certain table for coffee and fellowship following the service. He and his wife took up the challenge and congregated at the visitors' table. Despite their best efforts, after a couple of weeks this gregarious young couple were not made to feel particularly welcome. They left this church and continued their search for a friendly church family elsewhere.

Pastor Charles Mueller helped ailing and dying churches identify what has gone wrong and made suggestions for what a congregation could do to stem the tide of decline. Charles served as a school board member in our public high school district when I was school superintendent in suburban Chicago. He was also the pastor of a large congregation at Trinity Lutheran Church. Trinity Christian School is one of many continuing and influential ministries of this church. I learned a lot from Charles during his years of community service on our public high school district board.

Charles said that churches are either growing or they are dying. They do not remain in a status-quo mode. Churches can pay better attention to both "who" comes in the front door and "who" goes out the back door. Churches need to pay attention and to learn and care more about "why" individuals and families come in the front door and "why" some go out the back door.

Some churches copy our culture's corporate model of efficient impersonality. We emphasize structure and organization, which may negatively impact spontaneity and love for one another. Not so with the early church. The local church should be different than a corporation or some civic organization. Several years ago, David Mains shared in both his book *Full Circle* and within his Circle Church in Chicago that rather than try to get new people to fit into the existing church structure, we should alter the structure to allow people the opportunity to express in ministry the gifts given to them by God. Pastor Mains and his wife, Karen, said that the church needs to be more human, more interested in people.

Karen Mains reminded us of the importance of sharing our home environment and hospitality with others in her book, *Open Heart, Open Home.* Who do church members turn to in time of personal crisis? They seem as likely to turn to professional community organizations as to a pastor or church friends. We can work individually and together to be more helpful to those in need in our fellowship of faith.

The impersonality of our often-bureaucratic culture has infiltrated our churches. We often pay lip service to Christian values and behaviors, while in reality we often conform to cultural norms more than we might suppose. But we can make improvements. We can be positively distinguishable from those who are fully immersed in our culture. We can change in small and sincere ways at first—smile, say hello, initiate a short conversation, ask fellow parishioners about themselves, be an "unofficial greeter." Your greeter status will be recognized because of your inward thoughtfulness, not because of an external ribbon or carnation. I think informal greeters are the best kind.

For certain people and occasions, you may need to make a phone call, pay a visit, or write a letter or send a card of encouragement. Encourage *koinonia* or cell groups or small groups within the church where individuals can get to know one another better in a spiritual and social environment. This is always important, especially in a large church. And each of us can do little things on our own. Instead of always sitting with the same group and even in the same pew or same table during church functions, we can rather reach out to others and move around a bit.

If someone is in need, it is not really very helpful to say, "Call me if you need help." No one will call. Rather we could say, "I'll bring dinner Monday night," or "I'll drive you to the hospital tomorrow," or "I'll be over Saturday morning to help in any way I can." Or, "Can I pick you up Saturday and we can go to the game together?" It's about taking a small risk.

To be transformed in our relationships (Romans 12:2) requires that we treat people as whole persons—holistically. From witnessing to strangers to helping a friend in need, we are obligated to see people as total beings, people with fears, hurts, grudges, loves, ambitions. People fill many roles other than just church attendees; they are employees, parents, marriage partners, citizens, and taxpayers.

Like our larger culture, the churches have lapsed into a spectator activity. In society we passively watch sports instead of playing ourselves. We listen to Mandisa, TobyMac, Jamie Grace, Switchfoot, Chris Tomlin, Michael W. Smith, Kari Jobe, Britt Nicole, Francesca Battistelli, Lauren Daigle, MercyMe, Jeremy Camp, Matthew West, or other gifted Christian artists or groups instead of getting the family and friends around the piano and singing ourselves. It's okay to both sing and to listen to others sing. We listen and read what experts have to share instead of also thinking ourselves and seeking the wisdom and counsel of friends and using the brains God gave us.

The church of all places should be culturally transformed. We should be different in a good way. We should be a family of brothers and sisters who care for each other and for the world outside of our doors. We are told we will be known by our love for one another (John 13:34–35). Are we known for our love for one another? Perhaps the most damaging sin we demonstrate as Christians is that we are largely indistinguishable from the multitudes who are not Christians.

Members of a church family might lighten the load of fellow believers when their individual burdens become extensive. "Bear one another's burdens, and thus fulfill the law of Christ." (Galatians 6:2 NASB). Amish groups take this verse literally. For example, if a man loses his barn to a fire or a tornado, his friends and fellow Amish church members, without being asked, work together until a new barn is constructed. Breaks are taken during construction to eat food prepared at the work site by the wives and sisters and daughters. Due to this level of commitment to each other, Amish tend to feel that insurance, such as Social Security, is unnecessary. In practical ways we, too, are to help those in need (James 2:14–17).

We shouldn't confuse culture and lifestyle with true Christian piety. We often become offended when someone doesn't conform or comply with our cultural brand of Christianity. My wife and I were both church youth leaders when we were first married. It was a period of social upheaval during the Vietnam War, a time that included the so-called Jesus Movement. Our college-age youth group sponsored many activities, socials, and home Bible studies for fellowship, and in an effort to reach out to college-age kids who were not church attenders. The group successfully reached many with fellowship and the teachings of Jesus Christ. Several began to attend the regular services of the church, some were examining Christianity, and some were growing in their new faith.

One would think the church leaders would have been pleased with this outreach. Many of these new young seekers and Christians did not conform to accepted conservative clothing styles. And many had long hair, which really irritated several who served on the board of deacons. Sue Ann and I received some pushback. I was asked questions by church board members about why I was encouraging these "long-haired, possible troublemakers" to attend our church activities.

I tried to explain that they were not bad kids and while I personally didn't care much for long hair on males, it seemed a minor point. I explained that I thought we should be tolerant and accepting of others. Besides, isn't it more important what goes on inside of one's head rather than how long hair grows on the outside of one's head? Anyhow, many Christians throughout history had long hair. I was nervous talking with the board, but I even showed the board a picture of the great English preacher Charles Spurgeon. He was sporting long hair and a full beard.

It was of no use. The majority of the deacons had, in my view, fallen prey to the notion that their brand of conservative American culture, in this case, fashion, was somehow Christian. Several of these young people we were working with after a few weeks decided to leave the church. They said they did not feel welcomed. How can it be that we wouldn't welcome those who come to us? The witness of that church suffered because it majored on what was minor or even irrelevant and therefore had little time or spiritual energy left over for caring, loving, and accepting those who might be slightly different.

Do we need to gain victory over and insight into some cultural baggage that may hinder us from reaching out to others? Reading good books can help. Catherine Marshall wrote in *Something More* that we must release others from our judgment. In the process we release ourselves to be free to love others whom God leads into our lives. We are admonished to put aside cultural distractions and to accept one another (Romans 15:7) just as Christ has accepted us. Pastor Jerry Cook, in his book *Love, Acceptance and Forgiveness*, wrote how a church can truly reach out to others without letting cultural differences create adverse dissensions. The book, *Christianity Confronts Culture* by Marvin Mayers, while written for missionaries, is useful in helping any Christian "see" his or her culture more objectively. An influential book that exposes the secularization of American Christianity is *The Gravedigger File* written by Os Guinness.

Christians recognize that the church, like other institutions, can be adversely affected by culture. Lloyd Perry and Norman Shawchuck wrote about this in their book, *Revitalizing the Twentieth-Century Church*. I mentioned earlier David Murrow's book *Why Men Hate Going to Church*.[5] These authors discuss candidly the harsh and often unfair criticism that churches are boring, irrelevant, and full of hypocrites. These authors realize that the church has experienced interpersonal problems and cultural contamination, but with prayer and God's help and intimate fellowship and acceptance, the future will be better.

In Our Community and Country

Many Christians are uneasy with expressing their ideas in social settings even social situations within the church. It surely was not always this way. David Moberg from Marquette University in his book *The Great Reversal: Reconciling Evangelicalism and Social Concern* explains how Christians were active and influential in all areas of public and civic life until about 100 years ago. In our time many are reticent to engage the culture partially because of feeling unprepared or inadequate or wanting to be liked, and somewhat because of not wishing to offend another person.

It's okay, even important, to share your ideas and political and faith-based convictions. But we need to focus upon the issue at hand, not attack other people. Unless you can have a healthy exchange of ideas with someone, you don't experience interpersonal communication at its best. You need both honest interaction and real caring in a good relationship. In his book *Caring Enough to Confront*, David Augsburger lists how to care and confront at the same time.

Caring	Confronting
I care about our relationship.	I feel deeply about the issue at stake.
I want to hear your view.	I want to clearly express mine.
I want to respect your insights.	I want respect for mine.
I trust you to be able to handle my honest feelings..	I want you to trust me with yours.
I promise to stay with the discussion until we've reached an understanding.	I want you to keep working with me until we've reached a new understanding.
I will not trick. pressure, manipulate, or distort the honest view of our differences.	I want your unpressured, clear differences.
I give you my loving, honest respect.	I want your caring, confronting response.[6]

I have a shirtsleeve relative I see infrequently who is a committed Christian. This individual will not discuss any topic on which family members might possibly hold differing views. This is meant to keep relationships pleasant and pleasing to God. But the fact is, with this approach it's nearly impossible to even have much of a relationship. Communication is limited to only the exchange of trivial, superficial, safe comments, plastic smiles, and little else. How much better if we were all able to care and share and become a bit more trusting and honest with each other.

Robert Louis Stevenson said to travel hopefully is better than to arrive. We can acknowledge that our world is not and never will be perfect until Christ returns to this planet. Stan Mooneyham, former president of World Vision, recalled that John Bunyan did not title his book *Pilgrim's Destination* but rather *Pilgrim's*

Progress. We have not arrived. We need not be discouraged, but rather should work to improve the lives of individuals and the social institutions that greatly influence all of us.

We must have hope, and we can't succumb to fear and conspiracy theories and a sense that we lack opportunity and influence to help make for a better community and country. I hope we never give up on America or its people. Some Christians spend much energy with criticisms or conspiracy theories. Or they have given up mentally, deciding to sit out community involvement and just wait for the Second Coming. The parable of the savorless salt may apply to some of us today (Matthew 5:13).

Our nation is suffering from a decline in biblical values and influence similar to the period of Jewish history when "every man did that which was right in his own eyes" (Judges 21:25 KJV). The result for America has been moral decline, injustice, and even flashes of political chaos. The angry voices on both the political left and the right are getting louder.

During a time when CBS television received widespread criticism for the sex and violence presented in its programs, then CBS vice president Arnold Becker, made a revealing and disconcerting statement:

> I'm not interested in culture. I'm not interested in promoting social values. I have only one interest—that's whether people watch the program. That's my definition of good; that's my definition of bad.

Without a moral foundation, a nation usually degenerates into a state of spiritual and political anarchy. Humans cannot long endure chaos where everyone does his or her own thing, where everything is said to be relative and there exist no absolutes. The absence of a national structure of agreed-upon values ultimately leads to revolution and perhaps even dictatorship. This pattern has been repeated over and over in world history.

Writing at the beginning of the last century, Union Seminary professor and theologian J. Gresham Machen said you can remove the engineer from a locomotive and witness little initial impact. The train may coast for several miles before eventually stopping. In America, with a crisis of leadership and morality, we may coast for several years, even several decades. Eventually, however, a day of reckoning will occur.

Time magazine reported way back in the 1970s that at least 40 million people in America said they were "born again." Wikipedia recorded that there were 90 million American evangelicals in 2018. Shouldn't these many millions have a significant impact on our culture? With many millions of Christians, it should be possible and probable to influence our culture for good and for God. *The Living Bible* paraphrases Romans 12:2 as follows: "Don't copy the behavior and customs of this world, but be a new and different person with a fresh newness in all you do and think." We can influence our culture, especially in a free society based upon our greatly valued democratic form of government.

The writer in 2 Chronicles 7:14 recorded the Lord's conditions for cultural and spiritual change: "If my people, who are called by my name, will humble themselves and pray and seek my face and turn from their wicked ways, then I will hear from heaven and will forgive their sin and will heal their land." Many Christians know that even one person's influence can impact for good the social world of the early twenty-first century.

Christians may hold different views on the issues that confront us and how to solve our nagging and perplexing social, economic, and political problems. When we form friendships and with our dependence on Scripture, prayer, and the direction of the Holy Spirit, we individually and collectively can influence for good this great nation.

Christians disagree with each other on some issues, but we likely agree on many of the essential issues of our day. Assuredly we can all agree to be caring, concerned men who reach out to people in need. The lesson of the Samaritan is that we are not taking time from our lives when we befriend others; rather we are, in the midst of our lives, living our lives and caring for others to the fullest.

Discussion Questions

1. Moses rejected Egypt's lifestyle. What aspects of America's culture should we reject?

2. With many millions of evangelical Americans, why do they not have more of a positive spiritual impact on the American culture?

3. How do Christ's masculine traits differ from your own? What ideas do you have to help you better conform to Jesus' example on how to behave?

4. List some positive ways we can positively affect our culture with a biblical masculinity.

5. How can we distinguish cultural beliefs from Christian faith? Which ones are cultural, and which are really Christian?

Chapter 13

How Women Can Help?

Be faithful in little things because it is in them that your strength lies.
—Mother Teresa

At the still point of the turning world.
—T. S. Eliot

The message of this chapter is for the women in your life including your wife, or your sister, girlfriend, friend, or mother. I hope you will share this chapter with the important women you know and solicit their support as you work to enhance the quality of your relationships with others. I hope you will read the chapter too.

Admittedly men are not always easy to understand. And we are sometimes difficult to relate to. In every generation, there are several best-selling books and articles and now also online and social media sources that attempt to define the problems that beset men in relationships and provide suggestions on how to both understand and relate to men better.

A common thread throughout these publications is that men are not very well adjusted, they are unwilling to form committed relationships with women or other men, and women themselves are not to blame for the interpersonal relationship problems confronting men.

There is also another more conservative perspective that offers advice on how to keep the man in your life happy, such as massage his ego, say only what he wants to hear, pretend to be what he wants you to be, and indulge his every whim. In these publications, women are told to submit to their man.

These are different views published about how women and men might get along better. Each generalization contains simplifications met to serve either a conservative or liberal audience. The theories and suggestions often break down in the real world of complex problems and daily living. For example, when a woman is unable, despite her efforts and good intentions, to measure up to some superwoman syndrome, guilt and eventually anger may well set in. Women and men both need a balanced approach that doesn't need to take sides but rather looks for ways to honor each other and serve each other.

Thoughtful marriage counselors are quick to say that a marriage partner cannot meet all of one's emotional and spiritual needs. A marriage is healthier when both spouses lead integrated lives that includes friends. In cases where you find a man who says, "My wife is the only true friend I can turn to," you will also usually find a wife who says, "I only wish he'd find a friend." A wife cannot easily satisfy all the emotional and spiritual needs of her husband; nor can he meet all of hers.

As a man, I tend to want to reject this idea. I want to think I can meet all the needs my wife might have. Grudgingly, however, I must admit that I cannot be all things to even one person. While I believe that a husband and wife should be the closest of friends and the marriage relationship is far more important than any other kind of friendship, there is nevertheless room for and a need for men to form and maintain friendships with other men.

Just in case of any misunderstanding, I should emphasize that friendships outside marriage, while important, must not interfere with family activities. A husband and wife's principal responsibility is to each other and to their children. We need to protect our family's time together and not allow a friendship to siphon away inordinate amounts of time and energy from the family. Close friendships established on the biblical model realize the importance of the marriage and family relationships, and therefore do not permit the friendship to compete or interfere with family responsibilities.

When I was a guest on psychologist Dr. James Dobson's *Focus on the Family* radio program, I was asked several different ways if my emphasis on the importance of friendships among men might in any way negatively affect family life. To each question my answer was "no." Friendship should complement marriage and family life, not in any way compete with it for attention.

Friendships, like service in the community and church, can help make a man a better father and husband, as long as the principal focus of his life remains his family. I shared with Dr. Dobson from my heart my strong belief that men need friends, and if those relationships are biblical, they will enhance rather than detract from the marriage and family relationship. Husbands, as well as wives, need quality friendships to add balance and sharing to their way of living.

How can you help the man in your life develop close interpersonal relationships with other men? I asked many women to respond to this question on a questionnaire, and I received the following answers from most respondents:

- Encourage him to see his friends in our home; allow him time.
- Encourage him to reach out, to be more personal, to do things with other men.
- Create an atmosphere in which he is free to grow as a person.
- Let him know it's not a crime to let his feelings show.

- I need to point out his good qualities. I need to draw him out more, to listen more and to get him to express his feelings.
- We could do more together with other couples from our small group at church.

Almost without exception, these women believe it is important to encourage their men to develop positive male relationships. Encouragement is the theme of this chapter, for active encouragement is the way you will best help your husband with his interpersonal friendships. This, of course, is also true for any important man or young man in your life such as your father, brother, nephew, or son. The rigidity of the macho male role hinders growth of close friendships. Psychotherapist Edward B. Fish is of the opinion that macho men would disappear like snowballs in July if women stopped making it so easy for them. I don't know if this is true for many women, but for sure each woman can look for ways to reinforce and encourage what we might refer to as "better behavior."

You can help your husband set priorities for his activities and behavior that coincide with biblical values. Jerry and Mary White in their book *The Christian in Midlife* share that all too often a man awakens too late and discovers that his family and friends have lived for years in the shadow of his work and ambitions. Wives can encourage husbands to lead a more enjoyable, balanced life that includes, work, recreation, church, community service, family, and friends.

Establish a Balance

The more a man centers his identity in just one phase of his life, such as his vocation, the more vulnerable he is to threats against his identity and the more prone he is to experience a personal crisis. A man who has limited sources of identity is potentially the most fragile. Help your husband to recognize and experience his different selves. If your husband tends to become overly intellectual during discussions, you may want to ask how he feels about the topic at hand. Give him the freedom to express his inner feelings. Make sure you don't reject his feelings, however, once you begin to hear them. It's okay to be silly and moonstruck—listening together for example to an "oldie but goodie" tune—and then a moment later, seeing life passing by, to launch into an intellectual or spiritual discussion about life's meaning. Different moods and emotions complement our lives.

Encourage the man in your life to be a well-rounded human being. Many sad people are too concerned with themselves or their jobs rather than with their families and friends. Some men and women talk about an identity crisis—"I don't know who I really am." They fail to grasp the biblical principle that identity comes not from focus on self, but from concern for and relationships with other people.

It's currently fashionable with some to minimize relationships that require commitment, such as those with parents, marriage partners, children, and friends. With men who lack commitment we can refer to them as "Peter Pans." I don't know if we have a comparable term for women who lack commitment. A thirty-three-year-old woman with two very young daughters from her ten years of marriage found a lover online, which led to her demanding a divorce. Her explanation was "I want what I want, and I want to be free to be myself." The end of such immaturity and selfishness is usually frustration, poverty, shame, and sadness. Inordinate immature selfishness that is fairly common in the West is still rare in some cultures, where family, friends, and even the community may come before the individual. The irony is, the more self-centered one becomes in the pursuit of their own happiness, the less likely they will ever discover real happiness.

Women can build the confidence of their husbands and encourage their development as well-rounded human beings. To do this requires that men commit themselves to others. Men especially need the mature love and devotion only their wives can give. I'm convinced that there is nothing more important to a man than to know that his wife truly cares for him and respects him.

While I was conducting research for this book, one forty-one-year-old man I interviewed told me, "I work with men under stressful situations. These guys don't know how to express emotions. My wife has taught me to bring my feelings out. I'm a better man today because of her. She really cares about me."

In my own life, some say that my outgoing nature is largely the result of the rich, supportive relationship I enjoy with my wife, Sue Ann. I agree. Without her love and genuine concern for my welfare, I'm sure I'd be a different person. Maybe it's the little boy that remains in all men. Whatever it is, I know that every man will respond positively to genuine concern and caring affection. We need the constant support of the woman we love. Sue Ann not only tells me she loves me, she gives specific reasons for her love. This is one of the greatest things a wife can do for her husband. With support from a spouse and from friends, a man is more likely to be outgoing and concerned about others. Encouragement at home helps a man develop his identity to his full potential.

Don't Expect Too Much

Many men, despite acquiring chronological adult status, remain little boys at heart. Theodore I. Rubin was a popular monthly columnist for the *Ladies Home Journal*. What Rubin said long ago remains true today. He said American society tends to produce mature women, but for some reason many men remain little boys with traits such as abnormal insecurity, frustration, jealousy, insensitivity, and apprehension. Rubin believes women need to know that many men:

- Retain more of the "little boy" than women do the "little girl."
- Don't like to admit they are dependent.
- Are fearful, jealous, and contemptuous of women.
- Will not admit to soft, warm feelings that they consider feminine.
- Feel they must be strong, that is, stubborn, and competitive.
- Are unable to establish mature man-to-man friendships because of a fear of homosexuality.
- Have difficulty relating to children; because of their own childlike characteristics, they see their own children as competitors for their wife's affection, time, and energy.
- Are unable to measure up to masculine ideals and are prone to self-depreciation.
- Won't admit that they crave affection; men want to be coddled and fussed over, especially in stressful times.
- Are vulnerable to vanity and concerned with looking young and sexually appealing.
- Measure self-esteem in terms of power and money.
- Fear loneliness even more than women; many men are afraid of leisure time and vacations and do not adjust well to retirement since most of their psychological support is derived from work.
- Are frightened by the possibility of rejection by women.[1]

Men are a little different and perhaps a little strange. They are unpredictable, illogical, and often seem a bit crazy. You might consider allowing your man a little weirdness in harmless areas. Don't always require an explanation for everything. He won't always be able to provide one. Be as realistic as possible. In your effort to help him help himself, don't expect miracles. Human behavior for both men and women is difficult to change. This is true for either positive or negative behavior. So don't expect too much too soon. Our society has placed confusing expectations on married men, demanding that they be all things to all people, including the capable provider, the aggressive competitor, the wise father, the sensitive and gentle lover, the fearless protector, the controlled one under pressure, and the emotionally expressive person at home.

Men change slowly in their relationships if they change at all. Billy Graham used to say he was amazed by men who spend days successfully analyzing a problem in their business and yet seem unwilling or incapable of analyzing what is wrong with either their marriage or friendships.

Men spend their days with men they must compete with or who are of either a higher or lower work status. Women must also compete with coworkers, but women are more likely and able to establish satisfying relationships and even friendships with their coworkers.

Donna, a woman about forty years old, told me that criticism is deadly to a marriage relationship, especially if it's done in the presence of relatives, neighbors, or friends, or as gossip behind the husband's back. She had learned over the course of her marriage that criticism is deadly to the male ego. Donna said, "I'm the one who creates the emotional tone of our home. I respect his friends and try to take at least some interest in his relationships with them."

Women are more likely to take the initiative in relationships, and they usually reap the benefits of being concerned about others as well. I worked once as an adult education director. The best teacher to work in that program was a woman named Elizabeth Jacobson. She was not only an excellent teacher, but she truly cared about and was available for her adult students. There was a time when Elizabeth's then fourteen-year-old daughter, Karen, was injured severely in a motorcycle accident. Elizabeth said, "I cannot hide my emotions. I spent most of the past few weeks in tears, but I didn't cry alone. There always seemed to be someone there for me. I felt neither alone or afraid." Elizabeth was grateful for her friends and loved ones in this time of need. But there was another source of comfort.

There were strangers at school and at the hospital who reached out. Elizabeth remembers the outreach from her own adult students and parents of Karen's classmates and from others who were strangers. There were offers to help from mothers whose children had been similarly hurt. Some called, some wrote, some simply came to me to say, "Aren't you Elizabeth? I also have a child who had a similar experience." Elizabeth remembers "that on one particularly upsetting visit to the hospital, a woman I had never met approached me and asked, 'Are you Karen's mother?' When I nodded, she said she had something to give to me—and she wrapped me in her arms." This woman's son had lost his leg and was lying in a hospital bed with brain injuries from a motorcycle accident. She had also lost another son three years earlier in another accident. And still, this woman, whose loss was greater than Elizabeth's, wanted to comfort her.

Women who reach out, who make the effort first to talk and care, are not doormats for the men in their lives. The opposite is true. Women who care and share with strangers, friends, and family alike enrich their own lives and the lives of others who know them. This is the way all of us should live, men included! It's less about what is masculine or feminine behavior and more about what is good and positive and helpful behavior.

In 1937, Dale Carnegie wrote a book that quickly sold eight million copies, I suppose because his advice was so practical. Some may argue that his *How to Win Friends and Influence People* after over eighty years is dated and doesn't fit life as we live today. But his ideas are useful today and for the most part, founded on biblical principles. According to Carnegie, "the best way to make more and lasting friendships is to get your mind off yourself and to take a genuine interest in other people. Be generous and sincere with praise when you see positive changes. Don't be critical of another's behavior. It only makes them defensive. Rather, get them or him to express their ideas. Listen to their ideas and be respectful of them even if you don't fully agree with what's being said."

Good advice for everyone, men and women alike. We need to value and give our attention to the development of the internal things of the heart and spirit. The point of 1 Peter 3:1–6, for example, is that jewelry, clothes, cosmetics, and other externals are not very important despite what we hear daily from newspaper, radio, television, and social media. A primary emphasis on the physical external things will do little either to build a good marriage or help husbands form quality friendships.

A Positive Role Model

Before you can help a man develop friendships, your own relationship with him needs to be a good one. You must be a trusted confidante, one he feels free to turn to in time of need. And even then, unfortunately, you can't expect him to change directly overnight. Our influence upon others results only indirectly, so if we want someone else to change, we must first look at our own behavior. Talk alone won't usually bring about change. It'd been said by many that "talk is cheap." People can be won over without a word due to one's manner of life. In fact, a man can hardly be changed in any other fashion.

Women can be assertive in a thoughtful way, which may lead a husband to a changed life. This occurred dramatically in my own life. Typically, I followed the crowd during my teen years. I had no real plans or goals of my own that I would have been able to identify. Frequently I found myself in academic trouble in school, causing my mother concern. My father had died when I was only twelve.

After three semesters in college, I found little that interested me, so I dropped out. My lifestyle didn't bother me, but I knew I had very little purpose in my life. It never occurred to me that I might be missing out on something—until I met Sue Ann and her family. It didn't take long for me to see that she was different. I was particularly impressed with her family. Her mother was perhaps the most wonderful person I have ever met. I saw a genuine concern for others and a quiet confident spirit in her mom's life, and also in Sue Ann's life.

One afternoon, she told me what made her life special. She said being a Christian was a matter of having faith in what Christ had done for us. I couldn't do enough good works to earn my way to God. No one could. But Jesus Christ had died for my sins. She shared a few Scripture verses, including Ephesians 2:8–9: "For it is by grace you are saved, through faith and this is not from yourselves, it is the gift of God." And then the verse in Titus 3:5 (KJV): "Not by works of righteousness which we have done, but according to his mercy he saved us." Somehow everything she told me and the Scripture she shared with me all made sense.

Our discussion influenced me. Later when I was alone, I realized I needed God in my life. I prayed and asked God to forgive my sins, and by His grace, to help me become a better person. My life was changed. God gave me contentment in place of restlessness. He gave me purpose in place of aimlessness. He exchanged my apathy for a thirst for knowledge. In the words of C.S. Lewis, I was "surprised by joy." God really did change me. Several months later Sue Ann and I were married. Why did I respond to her sharing with me from Scripture and from her life? It wasn't just her words really; it was the way she lived her life. The way she lived led me to want to hear her words.

In the musical *My Fair Lady*, the character Henry Higgins asks, "Why can't a woman be more like a man?" This is one of my favorite musicals, but I think the question would be more appropriate if reverse: "Why can't a man be more like a woman?"

From the surveys I conducted, women seem more prepared to make and keep friends than men.

Major on the Majors

Stay on track and don't get distracted. Perhaps you recall the time when Christ, on his journey to Jerusalem, stopped at the home of Martha and Mary. Jesus needed human fellowship as He contemplated the agony of His anticipated suffering and death. Mary listened to Jesus as He spoke. But Martha was distracted by all the preparations that had to be made. And Martha apparently resented her sister's seeming idleness. Martha said, "Lord, You do not care that my sister has left me to serve alone?" Jesus responded directly, "Mary has chosen that good part" (Luke 10:38–42).

Martha's concern with the meal is, of course, not wrong in itself. We all have to eat. Both sisters loved Jesus and were doing what they thought best at the moment. But timing and priorities must be considered. Evangelist D. L. Moody's observation was that the good is often the enemy of the best. This was true for Martha during Jesus' visit. We need to guard against and be aware of the barren, busy life. Perhaps women are more susceptible to this circumstance because of the endless tasks that must be accomplished with work and home and community and other responsibilities. We all can be profitably reminded to set lesser matters aside frequently and concentrate upon developing and nurturing an in-depth relationship with loved ones and others too.

Look for areas of interest you and your husband share that you can engage in together. Listen to each other. Take a long drive and talk about anything and everything. Schedule a break in the routine. Have breakfast together. Walk or exercise together. Have devotions or Bible study together. Read some of the same magazines and books and share ideas together. Plan to spend some time together each day without distractions.

Plan for the Future

Kids make friends easily. When my family moved into a community near Indianapolis, our then eleven-year-old son, Cameron, had made friends with several of the neighborhood children even before our furniture and other belongings were off the moving van. Children seek personal bonds because of a need for love and companionship. Only later do they learn to suppress these needs. Parents can subtly influence their kids, especially boys, to not be so outgoing.

"The hand that rocks the cradle is the hand that rules the world." Susanna Wesley never prepared a sermon or wrote a book, but she is remembered as the "Mother of Methodism" because two of the children she raised in faith nearly alone were John and Charles Wesley. For sure the way you rear a son or daughter now will directly influence his or her adult life. Sarah Pierpont married Jonathan Edwards, who later became the famous minister during the 1720s' First Great Awakening in colonial America. Sarah raised godly children and greatly influenced her husband. Sarah helped him become self-confident and gentler and improve his social skills. Jonathan grew closer to Christ because of Sarah's influence. You might Google "women of the faith," and you'll discover dozens of godly women who influenced their sons and daughters and husbands and their communities.

This is true in all cultures and within each of the world's approximately 196 countries. Margaret Mead, in her book *Sex and Temperament in Three Primitive Societies*, which I mentioned earlier, pointed out that a strong association exists between child-rearing practices and later personality development. Children who received a good deal of attention and gentleness, as among the New Guinea mountain Arapesh, became cooperative, unaggressive, friendly adults. But children of the New Guinea Mundugomor community, who were raised with perfunctory and intermittent attention, developed into uncooperative, aggressive, and unfriendly adults. The Bible records in Proverbs 22:6, "Train up a child in the way he should go and when he is old he will not depart from it."

Sue Ann wrote a letter to our son when he was in second grade. She gave it to him when he got older. In those early years, she had been teaching Cameron to be affectionate and loving, even when it might be inconvenient.

> Dear Cameron:
> It was a typical cold late November day today. Your friends Ken and Kristy stopped over to wait with you for a few minutes before the school bus arrived to chauffeur you to North Elementary School and to Mrs. Jellison and your second-grade classroom.
> You announced, "Mom, the bus is coming," and out the door you and your friends went to face the world and to be the first in the bus line. Thirty seconds later you returned, rushed back into the house, up the steps, and to the window where I had been watching you. In your hurry you had forgotten to kiss me good-bye before you left. You kissed me and left again quickly and returned to your friends.
> We started most of your school days with kisses and prayers. This is the way it should be, even if you lose your place in line at the bus stop. Thanks for coming back to give me a kiss, son. You made my heart smile.
> Love, Mom

What you do with and for children will have lasting influence. Do we relate differently to our sons than we do our daughters? What do you think? Should you teach them differently? What do we and should we say to our kids about gender issues? Do we discourage our sons from expressing feelings and emotions with a "boys don't cry" attitude or comment? You can make sure your son and daughter rotate tasks such as dishes, gardening, lawn mowing, and cleaning the cat box so that these jobs are not viewed as gender-oriented. What impact will certain toys or video games have on our children? What are your kids reading at school and for leisure on their smart devices? Does any of this reading material possibly reinforce distorted images of what is manly?

An important method of helping both sons and fathers develop relationship skills is to encourage fathers to take more of the child-rearing responsibilities. By spending more time with his children, a man will acquire an ability to express his emotions more fully, and the sons along with daughters will learn that it's very normal for a dad to spend quality time with his children.

Men have a need to nurture. Women can help their men create a balance between kids and careers and thus become better husbands, fathers, brothers, and sons. And they can become better friends too.

Discussion Questions

1. How can you positively impact another person's behavior indirectly?

2. In what ways, like Martha in Luke 10, are you distracted from developing better communication and relationship skills?

3. Using God's promise about child rearing from Proverbs 22:6, discuss the extent of our influence and responsibility as parents in helping sons develop wholesome friendships.

CHAPTER 14

The Caring of Friendships

As surely as the Lord lives and as you live, I will not leave you.
—Elisha to Elijah, 2 Kings 2:2

A man must get friends as he would get food and drink for nourishment and sustenance.
—Randolph S. Bourne

During one of the executive school district searches I was conducting, an assistant superintendent I had worked with had just been passed over by a school board for the superintendent position. A new man had been brought in from the outside. The assistant superintendent was displeased, but the new superintendent needed the support and friendship of this assistant superintendent.

"As tough as it might be," I told the unhappy assistant, "I would keep your wounded ego to yourself and walk into that new superintendent's office and with committed sincerity let him know you want to help him in every way possible." In conversation with the assistant, I told him he could acknowledge his disappointment with the new superintendent but also let him know that he was now his supporter and a team player. I told him the new superintendent needs him and so did the school district. He continued to listen as I advised that he practice empathy and put himself in the new person's shoes and also try to practice the

Golden Rule: "Do unto others as you wish they would do unto you." I said, "It will pay off all the way around."

Thankfully the assistant superintendent buried his pride and hurt feelings and applied the Golden Rule in working with his new boss. As a result, the two men established a good working relationship. Four years later the superintendent moved on to another district. You guessed it. Before leaving, the departing superintendent recommended to the school board that the assistant superintendent succeed him. I didn't get to conduct the board's search for a new superintendent because the assistant got the head job and this time a search wasn't necessary. The new superintendent has a framed legend on his office wall listing the "Golden Rule." The two men learned to depend upon each other and developed a warm, working relationship that was a benefit to many, including themselves.

Unfortunately, in business and the public sector many learn early to look out only for number one as they fight their way up some professional ladder. A friend of mine, who is a superintendent of schools, has discovered it is difficult to develop warm working relationships with coworkers. Some coworkers are fearful, suspicious, or critical of him and his decisions because of his position of responsibility. Thankfully there are a few exceptions to this, but overall, he feels somewhat alone at work. To meet the need for camaraderie, many superintendents and others with management responsibilities find it useful and refreshing to meet once a month for lunch, discussion, and fellowship with others who hold similar positions.

Dozens of studies have been conducted to find out why some people are happy and others are unhappy. The findings are very consistent. One criterion is that those who are happy are more likely to live in the present and future but not the past. Happy people do not waste time and energy fighting conditions that cannot be changed. And happy people are concerned about others.

Contented people, instead of complaining about not having good relationships, seek rather to enter into the lives of others. I've mentioned before, when you involve yourself in someone's life, you take risks; you're vulnerable, or at least you feel vulnerable. This risk taking is even evident with seemingly minor things in life such as writing a letter or even an email or text message. Sometimes we can reach out and take a small risk. Take the slight chance that you will be rejected, because to do otherwise may be to miss some of the greatest joys of life and to contribute in some meaningful way to the lives of others.

Early in the history of our republic, the significant sacrifice and wisdom of both John Adams and Thomas Jefferson helped to establish the new American nation. While both men shared a love for the new United States of America, these two Founders had lost affection for each other. Some historians think that the arrogance and abrasive personality of John Adams contributed to the falling-out with Jefferson. The political and personal hostility was very noticeable when, following Jefferson's election in 1800, Adams chose not to attend the new president's inauguration.

Years passed. There was a complete lack of communication between these two essential founding statesmen for nearly twenty-five years. Long after Jefferson's two terms, when Jefferson was sixty-eight and Adams was seventy-five, a brief letter from Adams arrived at Monticello, Virginia. Adams simply stated that he and his family were well. It wasn't the content that mattered but rather the signature that gladdened the heart of Thomas Jefferson. The letter was signed, "With sincere esteem, your friend and servant, John Adams." This simple letter initiated a wonderful and warmhearted correspondence between two great Americans.

Time had blunted the sharp edges of the political differences. Now later in life, with both in retirement, they could resume a friendship that was started back when they were both comparatively young rebels against the British Empire. Adams wrote in one of his first letters to Jefferson he felt strongly that, "We ought not to die before we have explained ourselves to each other." Isn't that a wonderful thought and suggestion? I think that comment is so important, so meaningful. Adams took a risk and hoped for a good response. I wonder today where I should take a risk and reach out to someone and anticipate a good outcome.

It was John Adams's wife, Abigail, who approached Dr. Benjamin Rush, also one our Founders and a signer of the Declaration of Independence, and an admirer of both Adams and Jefferson. Abigail prevailed upon Dr. Rush to bring the two together, to get them both to "chill out." Abigail Adams had an essential role in the reconciliation of the two Founders. Dr. Rush encouraged Adams to write to Jefferson. Of the 158 letters of correspondence that followed between the two men from 1812 to 1826, Saul Padover says, "The two old gentlemen, both men of massive learning and vast intellectual curiosity, poured out their ideas with the zeal and zest of youngsters. To the intimacy of their letters they entrusted their innermost hopes and fears and prejudices and convictions and indignations."[1] Pulitzer Prize–winning historian Gordon Wood concludes that Rush had maintained for decades a friendship and mutual respect with these two very different Founding Fathers.[2] Benjamin Rush left us a good example about bringing individuals together. Without the concerned intervention of Dr. Rush, both Adams and Jefferson would have missed the joy that resulted from this noble fellowship.

We can suffer strain in our relationships and refuse to seek reconciliation—until it's too late. The headline read *Feuding Brothers Die on Same Day*. In Dedham, Massachusetts, two brothers who had rarely spoken to each other in twenty-five years died within two hours of one another in the same emergency room. The wife of one of the brothers said that her husband was on the verge of making peace with his brother and had told her the week before that he planned to phone his elder brother. Both died of heart attacks. They never made peace over a relatively minor family dispute that took place twenty-five long years before. How bankrupt our lives can become when we fail to reach out and sometimes to reconcile with others.

Before making a career move to suburban Indianapolis, my wife and I had met monthly with three other couples from our church for fellowship. Our times together were refreshing, spiritually and socially. Sue Ann and I remember well the good conversations, laughter, and on occasion the sharing of personal issues and concerns. A few months before Sue Ann and I packed our bags to move, one of these families moved to Massachusetts. We missed them and felt a sense of personal loss.

As I was preparing to write this book, I went through all my files looking for relevant material on the subject of relationships. In one folder I discovered a letter I had written to my friend who had moved to Massachusetts. In my letter I mentioned that we missed him and Jane and that I was looking for a new job. I wrote that Sue Ann had found a neighborhood women's Bible study and that the kids were doing well in school. I asked my friend if he liked his new graduate-level teaching position. I cited a few other insignificant facts and closed with "Give our love to Jane and the children." I signed the letter and then almost defensively added, "P.S. This is National Letter Writing Week. Men seem to need excuses to write."

What I have to admit is that the letter in my file is the original copy. I didn't send the letter. It's very difficult for each of us to understand our own emotions and the reasons behind our individual behavior, but I have an idea why David never received my letter. To begin with, I didn't believe the letter was very informative or intellectual. David is a few years older than me and very accomplished professionally. I suspect I didn't want to seem dumb and uninformed to this urbane gentleman whom I respect. Also, I didn't have much to say and therefore had no reason really to write. When you boil it down, one salient reason for not sending the letter emerges: I couldn't predict with any accuracy how he might react or respond to my letter, so I guess I refused to risk possible rejection.

A few months later, when Sue Ann and I were preparing for our move and change in jobs, she encouraged me to call David since he had recently struggled with a similar job change experience. I put it off. She persisted. When I finally did call, our conversation was quite enjoyable, and he gave me some ideas that helped my family deal with the new job transition I was then dealing with. But more important, the call helped to maintain a relationship. The lesson for me is to take the time and the risk with small things. This is how friendships begin and are maintained. Letters, phone calls, smiles, luncheons, talking and listening, helping, and countless other small activities are the building blocks to friendship.

Soon after arriving in our new community and beginning a new job for a suburban Indianapolis school district, I received two letters from friends with whom I used to work. I was thrilled to get both letters. John's letter began: "Hope you are settled in with your family and have not started too many new curriculum projects yet." He continued, "An old Jesuit once told me to distrust any man who wants to change something before he knows what it is." I appreciated my friend John's thoughtful advice.

The other letter also produced a smile as old memory were recalled and new information shared. This letter closed with the words, "I miss you, David." I appreciated so much this man's willingness to share with me the fact that I am important to him. He lifted my spirits with his acknowledgment of our friendship. There is a powerful tendency to like people who like us. If the greatest truths are usually the simplest, then this is one of them. We may think that it is the romantic, exciting, and adventurous actions that attract people, but more often it is the everyday, ordinary, even mundane, acts that determine and sustain a friendship.

Little things really are important, aren't they? We can express friendship in some small way, like writing a letter that really doesn't have to be written. I send emails and text messages, but I still use letter writing and phone calls for my most important personal communication. You may think of some other way that you feel comfortable with to connect to your friends. You'll feel better, and you may reap the rich dividends of closer, more nurturing, interpersonal relationships when you take the initiative.

Relationships are often won or lost in the first several minutes when we meet someone for the first time. When we meet someone, we are quick to form what become lasting impressions. First impressions are not always accurate. Major League knuckleball pitcher Hoyt Wilhelm hit a home run at his very first time at bat. But in his long twenty-year career, he never hit another home run. While first impressions are not always accurate, they are always important. The formula for success with new acquaintances during these critical minutes is not very complicated. We need to have direct eye contact and extend our hand as a greeting. Use the other person's name and ask sincere questions. And, of course, we need to smile.

Radio personality Earl Nightingale, of an earlier generation, said about meeting someone, "I'll make him glad he talked with me." Humorist Will Rogers once commented, "I never met a man I didn't like." From motivational speakers including Dale Carnegie to Zig Ziglar Tony Robbins and Eric Thomas, we learn that it's really not difficult to begin positive relationships with others, especially when we have the other person's best interest in mind. So I offer the following summary list to remind us to use these basic ideas during the first few minutes of meeting another person.

1. Introduce yourself.
2. Offer to shake hands.
3. Smile and look at the other person.

4. Listen actively to what the other person says.
5. Show sincere interest in the other person.
6. Remember and use the person's name.

Surely there will be people who will resist our smiles or offer of conversation. There may be individuals who will misunderstand our motive or will reject us and our interest in them. But these reactions should not deter us from our sincere efforts. The point is, when our attention is other person–centered and we resist the natural fears associated with risk-taking and we establish small, measurable goals, we often experience improvement in the quantity and quality of our relationships with others.

You can develop more valuable contact with other men and improve your relationships by introducing a few modest changes into your life. We shouldn't attempt unrealistic changes that will likely result in failure. I would encourage you to review both the biblical principles of friendship and personality traits associated with emotional intimacy listed below and discussed in Chapter 10. Then resolve to make daily small but real changes connected with these biblical and personality traits.

- God-centered consensus of beliefs
- Covenant
- Faithfulness
- Social involvement
- Self-disclosure
- Involvement
- Candor
- Respect
- Listening
- Acceptance
- Empathy
- Loyalty
- Compromise

For example, in reviewing the concept of involvement, you could resolve to in some way help another person each day. This could take the form of showing your appreciation for something someone had done. Maybe it would mean paying someone a sincere compliment or developing better listening skills. Maybe your involvement skill could be improved by sending a brief letter or email or text or making a phone call or visiting someone in your neighborhood or at the local retirement home. The point is to challenge yourself to do something you're not now doing. Start today. The dividends you'll reap will last for a lifetime for both you and individuals you connect with each day.

It's often the little things, like eye contact and other nonverbal signals, asking people questions, and saying thank you at the right time, that make or break a beginning relationship. Of the ten lepers healed by Jesus, one—only one—wasn't too busy to return to give thanks. Wow, only one guy took the time to express his thankfulness. Author Dale Carnegie said, "You can make more friends in two months by becoming interested in other people than you can in two years by trying to get other people interested in you."

A group of divinity students at Princeton University failed a "Good Samaritan" test because they were in too much of a hurry. Forty unwitting theology students were asked by researchers to go across campus for a special television taping session. On their way, the divinity students encountered a "victim" slumped in a doorway, coughing, groaning, and in apparent pain. Aware of a man in apparent distress, only sixteen of the forty seminarians stopped to help the man. The moral: A man in a hurry is likely to keep going and, in the process, miss opportunities for both service and important connection with other people.

A plaque entitled *A Friend* recently caught my eye. It read, "A friend is one who knows you as you are, understands where you've been, accepts who you've become and still gently invites you to grow." Our attitude about ourselves as well as about others is important. One of the important traits of emotional health is belief in your own likeableness. Another trait of emotional health is the corresponding belief that others are likeable too.

We must be aware that most people we meet in life are probably "okay." We know the biblical principle that all people are created and loved by God. We must, therefore, view all individuals as important and certainly worthy of our time and attention. Potential friends can be found anywhere.

Moving from one town to another can be a tough activity. Through the years we've been married, Sue Ann and I have moved about a dozen times. Accumulating all that is needed (or should I say wanted?) to keep a family functioning makes moving day complicated. Our move from Illinois to Indiana was a case in point. Three different neighbors whom we had helped move to nearby suburbs, learning of our anticipated departure, insisted on returning the favor. So, following two relatively expensive estimates from professional movers, we decided to do it ourselves. I accepted my former neighbors offers to help, as well as offers from some current neighbors.

The day before we loaded the orange U-Haul truck, Sue Ann and most—if not all—of the neighborhood women had a gigantic garage sale on our front lawn. It was a happening—buying, selling, and bartering more among each other than from the infrequent bona fide shoppers to our neighborhood flea market. Along with our neighbors, we laughed, and we were both happy and sad. The women had hugs and a few tears while the men resorted to hearty handshakes. In our seven years living in Northbrook, Illinois, we had developed many friends in a wonderful neighborhood.

Then, on our last night in town, Jerry and Dianna from our church called to say good-bye. After talking briefly, they said, "We're all going out for dinner." As tired as we were, it would have been easier to stay at home and order out. I'm glad we didn't. We had a great time during dinner. I'm also glad that we agreed to our neighbors' offers to help.

It's easy to avoid asking for or accepting help often because we can purchase our own things and services. I know it's better to give than to receive, but we don't need to be too stingy as receivers. After all, if I am a stingy receiver, then it's difficult for others to be givers. When we do everything ourselves, we cut off the potential for discovering and developing friendships. The result is a self-sufficient form of social isolation that may leave us lonely.

Not only did our family receive help in moving, but during our search for a new home in Indiana, we were fortunate to have the help and concern of two businessmen we met in our new town of Noblesville. At first, I was impatient with the pleasantries and later grew even skeptical of the kindness of these men. I wondered why our Realtor would invite us to his home for dinner and a neighborhood cookout. And when I introduced myself to a vice president of a local bank and began immediately to ask about interest rates for a needed mortgage and other related financial matters, the banker gently interrupted my inquiries with questions about my family, the move we just experienced, and my new position as a curriculum director for the local school district.

Then the banker said, "How do you like our town? Do you have any questions I might help with?" I finally slowed down to listen and even share something of myself. Finally, I came to realize that these men, while businessmen to be sure, were genuinely interested in my family. Long after we purchased our home, I continued to associate with these good men. The Realtor and the banker became friends. What's important is that they made an effort to be friendly, and I finally responded. With the hustle and bustle of house and mortgage hunting, and beginning a new job, it would have been easy to handle everything simply as business transactions, forgetting that potential friends can be found anywhere. This reinforced for me the simple yet important truth: "To have friends, be friendly."

Expand Your Comfort Zone

Potential friends can indeed be found anywhere if you're willing to be more aware of and open to men you have just met as well as those you have known for years. Even when we believe we are willing to form new friendships, usually we limit ourselves to the person who meets our very limited and narrow criteria of a possible friend. Friends tend to be selected from the same social class, race, political beliefs, faith-based background, and age range.

My father told me when I was very young that a man's character may be measured by the way he treats people who have little or no impact on his life. I have tried to remember and practice this principle, but not always successfully. What do we do when a stranger stops us and asks for money? I now carry a money clip with small bills always available when someone asks me for money. It is important to provide a generous gratuity for the good service we receive from those who provide much effort to serve us for usually low pay in hotels, restaurants, lawn care, nursing homes, retail sales, and housecleaning.3 Our thinking tends to be task-oriented, not people-oriented. We think of jobs to be done rather than individuals who need appreciation and recognition.

A retired milkman worked as a janitor in the high school where I taught history and social science classes for several years. We talked daily. Neither of us let the large difference in age and job roles keep us from enjoying each other's company. We even asked about each other's families and personal interests.

One day as we were talking, we both realized that this dear man, whom I called Mr. Hoffman, had known my father when they both worked for Borden Dairy on the north side of Chicago so long ago. We laughed and nearly cried as we explored this connection between us. He enjoyed sharing with someone who was interested. And it was a thrill for me to discover more about my father, who had died suddenly when I was very young. It's ironic that a principle my dad taught me was to be kind to others had helped to bring this good man into my life.

Another older man befriended me following my father's death. Lee gave me the time and attention I needed as an impressionable young teenager. He helped me land my first real job at Hoffman's Hardware Store. It was there that Lee took the time to teach me how to work and how to live up to my potential as a retail worker. He even sort of risked his life when he taught me to drive a car in a cemetery when I was fifteen years old. And I'll never forget his tolerance and kindness when, misjudging the length of a pier, I wrecked the front of his old wooden boat on a lake in central Wisconsin. He knew I felt badly about what happened. I learned a lot from this good friend, including that we don't need to let age differences get in our way of being friends.

Much of our socializing in America is done with people almost identical to ourselves. Diversity is sacrificed for similarity. Old people are isolated from the young. Rich and poor rarely meet or understand each other. Liberals and conservatives only shout at each other. The same is true for politics, religion, race, education, occupation, age, and marital status. It's as if we'll use any excuse to avoid connecting with a different kind of person.

An old people's home was constructed about a mile from the high school where I was teaching. Both buildings were off to themselves on the outskirts of a suburban town. In America, we seem to relegate both the young and old to an existence that is on the cultural sidelines. My students and I attempted to bring these two worlds together.

Our program was called YOU—Young and Old United. It was beautiful. The two age groups learned from each other. We got permission to conduct field trips for different events between our two institutions. In cultures where extended families still exist, people of different ages are able to learn from and contribute across the generations. Perhaps through groups like YOU and adopt-a-grandparent programs, we can reclaim an important extended-family type heritage.

People of different social or economic backgrounds rarely develop close relationships. This is somewhat understandable since diverse educational and income levels produce varied interests, predispositions, and opportunities. The Bible warns, however, against discriminating against people of a different social class, especially the poor. From the book of James, we learn that giving favored treatment to a man with wealth, while ignoring the poor man, is wrong (James 2:1–7).

Upon meeting someone for the first time, one of the first questions men ask is, "What do you do?" We want to know the other's social standing and level of learning. We hear the response to our question and then pigeonhole the person as someone to know better or someone not worth spending much time on. We get caught in the rut of equating the worth of a person with his occupation, wealth, and education.

American values have not changed a great deal since Vance Packard wrote *The Status Seekers* fifty years ago. The belief that what a man does for a living is the best measure of his worth as a human being is as false today as it was years ago. A man of great character may have a menial job, while someone with high status in his job may be dishonest or a failure as a parent or husband.

While researching social class differences for a college research project, I conducted some field work. My approach was what sociologists refer to as participant observation. For three days I arrived at 5:30 a.m. at a day labor-employment agency on the west side of Chicago. I was poorly dressed and unshaven. At about 6:00 a.m. each day my name was called, and I along with others were herded into a van and driven to a factory that needed extra short-term menial help. The work was tiring. I spent all day on an assembly line packing, of all things, rat poison. My pay was minimum wage. Almost no one talked to us except to give orders. Even eye contact was rare. It was as if we didn't exist. It was an eerie feeling to be largely ignored. Although I was in the old plant for only a few days, I had a strong desire to tell people "who I really was." Since that day-labor experience, I've wondered if any of those who ignored us were middle-class Christians. Each of us wants to be recognized, even by strangers.

A man, I'd guess about fifty years old, who also worked on the assembly line, sat down next to me in the day labor van at the end of the workday. He was dressed poorly and looked as if he had little of anything in this world or even a place to go. He smiled, looked me in the eye, said hello, and told me his name was Robert. And he asked me what my name was. I was tired and only thinking about my class assignment and had not expected this friendly greeting. I told him my name was David. He then reached into his pocket and pulled out a wrinkled paper bag that contained in waxed paper a sandwich of slightly stale white bread with peanut butter and grape jelly. Without hesitation he looked at me, smiled again, and handed to me half of his sandwich. I was surprised by his generosity but quickly accepted.

We then shared this modest early evening meal together and talked at first about not much of anything special. Robert smiled again and said, "I think you're new. How did it go today?" What followed was a real conversation where we shared and talked mainly about our workday. At the end of the ride, he looked into my eyes, smiled, shook my hand firmly, and wished me well. I thanked him again. Then he was gone. Robert reminded me of the angel Clarence from the 1946 classic Christmas film *It's a Wonderful Life*. I wondered, Had I just met an angel? I don't know if I met an angel, but I do know I will always remember Robert and I'll try to be more like him.

Robert gave me a sandwich, a smile, and friendly conversation, all during a van ride together. And he gave me much more. I learned anew that connecting with and concern for others, including strangers, can be normal and spontaneous. Generosity and kindness may come more easily from one who experiences poverty firsthand and feels personally the struggle. It is often those with the least who give the most.

Special people like Robert somehow let you know that their moment with you matters and is not just something on the way to something or someone else. I was reminded by Robert that good people can be found anywhere at any time and I need to be quick to receive kindness from others and to be ready to be kind to others. Kindness is the bridge between people. In a way, we are all just strangers on the bus (or van) in this life journey trying to make our way home. I want others to feel a little bit better off because of their time with me. It's really that simple. Robert reminded me how important is the Golden Rule and the need to treat others the way we want to be treated.

The power we have is not in our titles, our degrees, or our job description. Our strength comes from God and from our relationships with other people. Success is not worth a dime if it crowds out fellowship with and consideration for other people. If we crowd God and other people out, we are left largely only with regrets.

While friendships usually develop between people with related interests and backgrounds, I do believe we should relate to people as individuals, not as members of racial, economic, or social groups. Potential friends can be found in unsuspecting places—if you are willing to be open and to look.

There are millions of good people in this world, a few you work with or live near. I hope you will be open to them, perhaps get to know some of them better, be willing to discover their physical, emotional, and spiritual circumstances. The result can be warm, meaningful relationships and some friendships. The kindness you learn to extend to others will be returned sometimes many-fold. With God's help, we can become more consistently caring and concerned individuals.

Men need to view other men as individuals who have intrinsic worth and dignity as creations of God. And therefore, each person you meet is worth knowing at a personal level. There are two ways for men to follow through on these truths. First, a man must look for a need so that he can extend a hand of involvement. Second, a man must be willing to have some of his own needs met by others.

Can we stop trying to do everything by ourselves? And, at the same time, can we be more concerned with the needs of others? We will have a happier, more meaningful life if we can do so. Those who have your back are the very people who know they can count on you in both good times and bad. Friendship, like so many good things in life, comes to those who care for others. Best wishes as you continue the journey of making and maintaining quality relationships.

Discussion Questions

1. Do you have one or two close friends to whom you are committed by mutual agreement? If you must answer "no," how can you best begin to develop such a friendship?

2. When you first meet another man, by what criteria do you determine whether he could be a potential friend? Consider what occurs in the crucial first four minutes of a new relationship. What makes these four minutes so important?

3. Discuss other ideas for developing new friendships that may not have been mentioned in this chapter.

Notes

Chapter One: *Who Needs Friends?*
1. Phil McGraw, *USA Weekend* (February 1–3, 2013), 8.

Chapter Two: *Why Are We Lacking in Close Friendships?*
1. Viewpoint, *The Week* (December 17, 2013), 23.
2. Patrick Morley, *The Man in the Mirror* (Grand Rapids: Zondervan, 2014), 122.

Chapter Three: *The High Cost of Being Male*
1. Dev Aujla, *50 Ways to Get a Job: An Unconventional Guide to Finding Work on Your Terms* (New York: Tarcher Perigee Book, 2018).
2. Charles W Dunn, *The Nurse and the Navigator: A Son's Memoir of His Parent's Battlefield Romance* (New York: McNally Jackson, 2017), 125.

Chapter Four: *Basic Survival Needs*
1. Harold Kushner, *When All You've Ever Wanted Isn't Enough* (New York: Simon & Schuster, 2002), 18.
2. Victor Frankl, *Man's Search for Meaning* (Boston: Beacon Press,2006).
3. Kushner, *When All You've Ever Wanted Isn't Enough*, 92.

Chapter Five: *What's the Difference?*
4. John Gray, *Men Are from Mars, Women Are from Venus* (New York: Harper Collins, 2018).

Chapter Six: *Biblical Principles of Friendship*
1. Frances Schaefer, *The Mark of a Christian* (Downers Grove, IL: Intervarsity Press, 2007).

Chapter Seven: *Friendship Qualities We Look for in Others*
1. Lee Iacocca, *Iaccocca: An Autobiography* (Boston: G J Hill, 1985), 138.

Chapter Eight: *The Stages of Friendship*
1. Herb Goldberg, *The Hazards of Being Male: Surviving the Myth of Masculine Privilege* (Ojai, CA: Icon classics, 2006), 136.
2. Ambrose, Stephen, *Comrades: Brothers, Fathers, Heroes, Sons, Pals* (New York: Simon and Schuster, 2000), 106.
3. Patrick Morley, *The Man in the Mirror*, 293.

Chapter Nine: *Friendship in Other Times and Places*
1. Stuart Chase, *The Proper Study of Mankind* (New York: Harper & Row, 1956).
2. Aimee Byrd, *Why Can't We Be Friends? Avoidance Is Not Purity* (Phillipsbury, NJ: P & R Publishing, 2018).
3. John Fea, *Believe Me: The Evangelical Road to Donald Trump* (Grand Rapids: Eerdmans Publishing, 2018).
4. Robert Putzman, *Bowling Alone: Collapse and Revival of American Communities* (New York: Simon & Schuster, 2017).

Chapter Ten: *Understanding Yourself*
1. Sheryl Sandberg, *Lean In: Women, Work, and the Will to Lead* (New York: Alfred A Knopf, 2014).
2. C. S. Lewis, *The Four Loves* (New York: Harcourt, Brace, and World, 1960).

Chapter Eleven: *Setting Goals for Change*
1. O. Quentin Hyder, *The Christian's Handbook of Psychiatry* (Old Tappan, NJ: Fleming H. Revell Co., 1977), 144.
2. Jimmy Carter, *Faith: A Journey for All* (New York: Simon & Schuster, 2018), 106.

Chapter Twelve: *Confronting American Culture*
1. David Satter, "100 Years of Communism–and 100 Million Dead," *Wall Street Journal* (November 7, 2017), A17.
2. Ralph W. Keyes, "We the Lonely People," *Intellectual Digest* (December, 1973), 26.
3. Gary Collins, "Search of Christian Macho," *Moody Monthly* (July–August, 1976), 53–56.
4. "Dads Do Diapers and More, Myth Busting Survey Says," *Daily Herald* (January 6, 2014), A6.
5. David Murrow, *Why Men Hate Going to Church* (Nashville: Nelson Books, 2005).
6. David Augsburger, *Caring Enough to Confront* (Ventura, CA: Gospel Light, 2009), 15.

Chapter Thirteen: *How Can a Woman Help?*
1. Theodore I. Rubin, "What Women Don't Understand About Men," *Ladies Home Journal* (September 1973), 24.

Chapter Fourteen: *The Caring of Friendships*
1. Saul K. Padover, *Jefferson: A Great American Life and Ideas* (New York: Mentor Books, 1942), 163–164.
2. Gordon S. Wood, *Friends Divided: John Adams and Thomas Jefferson* (New York: Penguin, 2017).
3. Barbara Ehrenreich, *Nickled and Dimed: On (Not) Getting by in America* (New York: Metropolitan Books, 2017).

Invitation to Readers
Your comments, and suggestions related to *Who's Got Your Back?* are welcomed and can be sent to me at sds894@yahoo.com or David@FormingConnections.com. I can also be contacted for interviews or speaking at one of your faith based or leadership meetings or conferences at my email address or website www. FormingConnections.com.

Book Profits for Men's Ministry
Proceeds received by me from sales of this book are dedicated to men's ministry activities including those associated with *National Coalition of Ministries to Men.* NCMM.org

Printed in the United States
By Bookmasters